studysync®

Reading & Writing Companion

In Time of War

:::studysync®

studysync.com

Send all inquiries to:
BookheadEd Learning, LLC
610 Daniel Young Drive
Sonoma, CA 95476

Cover, ©iStock.com/bizoo_n, ©iStock.com/zabelin, ©iStock.com/alexey_boldin, ©iStock.com/
skegbydave

8 9 LWI 21 20   C

STUDENT
GUIDE

GETTING STARTED

Welcome to the StudySync Reading and Writing Companion! In this booklet, you will find a collection of readings based on the theme of the unit you are studying. As you work through the readings, you will be asked to answer questions and perform a variety of tasks designed to help you closely analyze and understand each text selection. Read on for an explanation of

CORE ELA TEXTS

In each Core ELA Unit you will read texts and text excerpts that share a common theme, despite their different genres, time periods, and authors. Each reading encourages a closer look with questions and a short writing assignment.

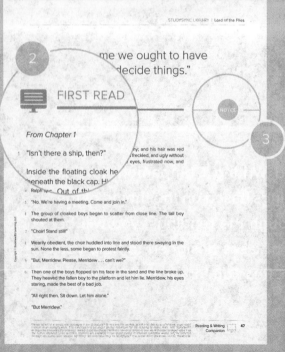

 INTRODUCTION

An Introduction to each text provides historical context for your reading as well as information about the author. You will also learn about the genre of the excerpt and the year in which it was written.

 FIRST READ

During your first reading of each excerpt, you should just try to get a general idea of the content and message of the reading. Don't worry if there are parts you don't understand or words that are unfamiliar to you. You'll have an opportunity later to dive deeper into the text.

 NOTES

Many times, while working through the activities after each text, you will be asked to **annotate** or **make annotations** about what you are reading. This means that you should highlight or underline words in the text and use the "Notes" column to make comments or jot down any questions you may have. You may also want to note any unfamiliar vocabulary words here.

4 THINK QUESTIONS

These questions will ask you to start thinking critically about the text, asking specific questions about its purpose, and making connections to your prior knowledge and reading experiences. To answer these questions, you should go back to the text and draw upon specific evidence that you find there to support your responses. You will also begin to explore some of the more challenging vocabulary words used in the excerpt.

5 CLOSE READ & FOCUS QUESTIONS

After you have completed the First Read, you will then be asked to go back and read the excerpt more closely and critically. Before you begin your Close Read, you should read through the Focus Questions to get an idea of the concepts you will want to focus on during your second reading. You should work through the Focus Questions by making annotations, highlighting important concepts, and writing notes or questions in the "Notes" column. Depending on instructions from your teacher, you may need to respond online or use a separate piece of paper to start expanding on your thoughts and ideas.

6 WRITING PROMPT

Your study of each excerpt or selection will end with a writing assignment. To complete this assignment, you should use your notes, annotations, and answers to both the Think and Focus Questions. Be sure to read the prompt carefully and address each part of it in your writing assignment.

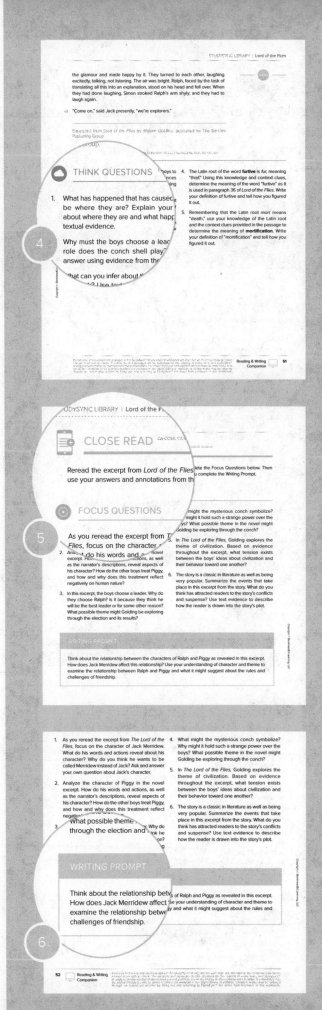

ENGLISH LANGUAGE DEVELOPMENT TEXTS

The English Language Development texts and activities take a closer look at the language choices that authors make to communicate their ideas. Individual and group activities will help develop your understanding of each text.

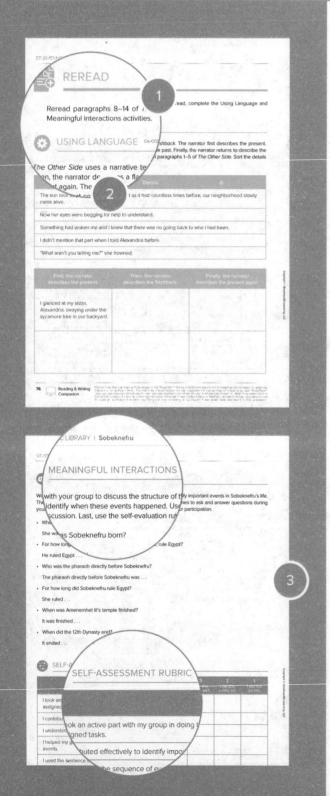

1 REREAD

After you have completed the First Read, you will have two additional opportunities to revisit portions of the excerpt more closely. The directions for each reread will specify which paragraphs or sections you should focus on.

2 USING LANGUAGE

These questions will ask you to analyze the author's use of language and conventions in the text. You may be asked to write in sentence frames, fill in a chart, or you may simply choose between multiple-choice options. To answer these questions, you should read the exercise carefully and go back in the text as necessary to accurately complete the activity.

3 MEANINGFUL INTERACTIONS & SELF-ASSESSMENT RUBRIC

After each reading, you will participate in a group activity or discussion with your peers. You may be provided speaking frames to guide your discussions or writing frames to support your group work. To complete these activities, you should revisit the excerpt for textual evidence and support. When you finish, use the Self-Assessment Rubric to evaluate how well you participated and collaborated.

EXTENDED WRITING PROJECT

The Extended Writing Project is your opportunity to explore the theme of each unit in a longer written work. You will draw information from your readings, research, and own life experiences to complete the assignment.

 ## WRITING PROJECT

After you have read all of the unit text selections, you will move on to a writing project. Each project will guide you through the process of writing an argumentative, narrative, informative, or literary analysis essay. Student models and graphic organizers will provide guidance and help you organize your thoughts as you plan and write your essay. Throughout the project, you will also study and work on specific writing skills to help you develop different portions of your writing.

 ## WRITING PROCESS STEPS

There are five steps in the writing process: **Prewrite, Plan, Draft, Revise,** and **Edit, Proofread, and Publish.** During each step, you will form and shape your writing project so that you can effectively express your ideas. Lessons focus on one step at a time, and you will have the chance to receive feedback from your peers and teacher.

 ## WRITING SKILLS

Each Writing Skill lesson focuses on a specific strategy or technique that you will use during your writing project. The lessons begin by analyzing a student model or mentor text, and give you a chance to learn and practice the skill on its own. Then, you will have the opportunity to apply each new skill to improve the writing in your own project.

UNIT 2   What does our response to conflict say about us?

In Time of War

TEXTS

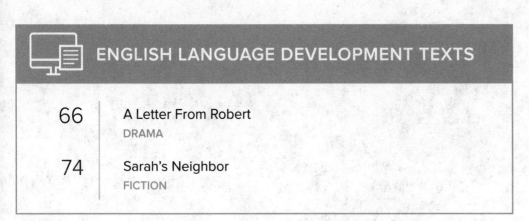

ENGLISH LANGUAGE DEVELOPMENT TEXTS

EXTENDED WRITING PROJECT

Copyright © BookheadEd Learning, LLC

BLOOD, TOIL, TEARS AND SWEAT

NON-FICTION
Winston Churchill
1940

INTRODUCTION

I n 1939, Great Britain found itself at war with Germany after the Nazi invasion of Poland. Hitler's army was raging across Europe, and British Prime Minister Neville Chamberlain was forced to resign. The First Lord of the Admiralty, Winston Churchill, a soldier and longtime critic of Chamberlain, took over as Prime Minister. In this speech before Parliament in May 1940, his first as Prime Minister, Churchill resolves to win the war by whatever means necessary. Inspiring the people of the United Kingdom to fight on, he borrows words first uttered in English by Theodore Roosevelt, "I have nothing to offer but blood, toil, tears, and sweat."

"We have before us many, many months of struggle and suffering."

 FIRST READ

 NOTES

1   On Friday evening last I received from His Majesty the mission to form a new **administration.** It was the evident will of Parliament and the nation that this should be conceived on the broadest possible basis and that it should include all parties. I have already completed the most important part of this task.

2   A war cabinet has been formed of five members, representing, with the Labour, Opposition, and Liberals, the unity of the nation. It was necessary that this should be done in one single day on account of the extreme urgency and rigor of events. Other key positions were filled yesterday. I am submitting a further list to the king tonight. I hope to complete the appointment of principal ministers during tomorrow.

3   The appointment of other ministers usually takes a little longer. I trust when Parliament meets again this part of my task will be completed and that the administration will be complete in all respects. I considered it in the public interest to suggest to the Speaker that the House should be summoned today. At the end of today's proceedings, the **adjournment** of the House will be proposed until May 21 with **provision** for earlier meeting if need be. Business for that will be notified to MPs at the earliest opportunity.

4   I now invite the House by a resolution to record its approval of the steps taken and declare its confidence in the new government.

5   The resolution:

6   "That this House welcomes the formation of a government representing the united and inflexible resolve of the nation to prosecute the war with Germany to a victorious conclusion."

7   To form an administration of this scale and complexity is a serious undertaking in itself. But we are in the preliminary phase of one of the greatest battles in

Please note that excerpts and passages in the StudySync® library and this workbook are intended as touchstones to generate interest in an author's work. The excerpts and passages do not substitute for the reading of entire texts, and StudySync® strongly recommends that students seek out and purchase the whole literary or informational work in order to experience it as the author intended. Links to online resellers are available in our digital library. In addition, complete works may be ordered through an authorized reseller by filling out and returning to StudySync® the order form enclosed in this workbook.

Reading & Writing Companion   **5**

history. We are in action at many other points—in Norway and in Holland-and we have to be prepared in the Mediterranean. The air battle is continuing, and many preparations have to be made here at home.

8   In this crisis I think I may be pardoned if I do not address the House at any length today, and I hope that any of my friends and colleagues or former colleagues who are affected by the political reconstruction will make all allowances for any lack of ceremony with which it has been necessary to act.

9   I say to the House as I said to ministers who have joined this government, I have nothing to offer but blood, toil, tears, and sweat. We have before us an ordeal of the most grievous kind. We have before us many, many months of struggle and suffering.

10   You ask, what is our policy? I say it is to wage war by land, sea, and air. War with all our might and with all the strength God has given us, and to wage war against a monstrous tyranny never surpassed in the dark and lamentable catalogue of human crime. That is our policy.

11   You ask, what is our aim? I can answer in one word. It is victory. Victory at all costs—Victory in spite of all terrors—Victory, however long and hard the road may be, for without victory there is no survival.

12   Let that be realized. No survival for the British Empire, no survival for all that the British Empire has stood for, no survival for the urge, the impulse of the ages, that mankind shall move forward toward his goal.

13   I take up my task in **buoyancy** and hope. I feel sure that our cause will not be suffered to fail among men. I feel entitled at this **juncture,** at this time, to claim the aid of all and to say, "Come then, let us go forward together with our united strength."

THINK QUESTIONS   CA-CCSS: CA.RI.8.1, CA.RI.8.4, CA.L.8.4a, CA.L.8.4b, CA.SL.8.1a, CA.SL.8.1b, CA.SL.8.1c, CA.SL.8.1d

1. According to the first three paragraphs of this excerpt of the speech, what has Winston Churchill been doing since becoming prime minister? Cite textual evidence to explain your understanding.

2. In the fourth paragraph, Churchill offers a "resolution" to the House of Commons in Parliament to "record its approval of the steps taken and declare its confidence in the new government." In paragraph six, Churchill states the resolution. What is he asking of the House? How important is this resolution? Explain your inference using evidence from the text.

3. What mood does Churchill convey as he moves through his speech? Use text evidence to explain how Churchill achieves it.

4. Use context to determine the meaning of the word **provision** as it is used in *Blood, Toil, Tears and Sweat*. Write your definition of *provision* and tell how you found it.

5. The Latin prefix *ad-* means "toward," and the root *jour* comes from the French, meaning "day." The Latin suffix *-ment* turns a word into a noun and has to do with an action or a process. Based on this knowledge of roots and affixes, write your definition of **adjournment** as it is used in the text, and tell how you got it. Use a dictionary to check its precise meaning.

CLOSE READ CA-CCSS: CA.RI.8.1, CA.RI.8.2, CA.W.8.4, CA.W.8.5, CA.W.8.6, CA.W.8.10

Reread the excerpt from *Blood, Toil, Tears and Sweat*. As you reread, complete the Focus Questions below. Then use your answers and annotations from the questions to help you complete the Writing Prompt.

 FOCUS QUESTIONS

1. Churchill asked the Speaker to summon the House today so he might deliver this speech. What makes the situation so important that this action must be taken right away? Highlight evidence from the text and make annotations to explain Churchill's main idea.

2. How does Churchill request that Parliament show its support for his actions? Highlight evidence from the text that shows Parliament's support of Churchill, as well as why it should continue its support. What do you think might have happened if the parliament had not given its full support? Use text evidence to support your inference.

3. Explain what Churchill means by the "monstrous tyranny never surpassed in the dark and lamentable catalogue of human crime." Cite textual evidence, as well as any of your own previous knowledge, to support your inference.

4. What is the central or main idea of Churchill's last five paragraphs? Highlight supporting details that help identify his central idea. State the central idea, and write a summary of the paragraphs.

5. Churchill is faced with an extremely difficult situation during his early days as prime minister. Compare the first half of his speech with the second half. What do both parts of the speech say about his strength as a leader in a time of war? Highlight textual evidence to support your answer.

WRITING PROMPT

According to Churchill's speech, what will war mean for the British people, and why should England be involved? How does the main idea of Churchill's speech reveal his response to conflict, and what does this say about him? Support your writing with textual evidence from the speech.

Reading & Writing Companion

ANNE FRANK: THE DIARY OF A YOUNG GIRL

NON-FICTION
Anne Frank
1947

INTRODUCTION

From a secret annex, Anne Frank wrote in her diary conveying the hopes and fears of an everyday teenager. But the times were anything but ordinary. The diary begins two days after Anne's 13th birthday, just 22 days before she and her family are forced into hiding, the occupying Nazi army scouring Amsterdam for Jewish people, loading them on trains to concentration camps. Her diary ends abruptly as she is betrayed and deported to Auschwitz. From there she is taken to Bergen-Belsen where she dies just two weeks before the concentration camp was liberated at the end of WWII. Of those who were in hiding with her, only her father Otto survived the war. He took on the task of editing and publishing Anne's unique journal, a perspective of a young girl amidst the unimaginable horrors of the holocaust. In the following passages, Anne's words portray her life both before

"...we're very afraid the neighbors might hear or see us..."

FIRST READ

WEDNESDAY, JUNE 24, 1942

1   Dearest Kitty, *nickname?*

2   It's **sweltering.** Everyone is huffing and puffing, and in this heat I have to walk everywhere. Only now do I realize how pleasant a streetcar is, but we Jews are no longer allowed to make use of this luxury; our own two feet are good enough for us. Yesterday at lunchtime I had an appointment with the dentist on Jan Luykenstraat. It's a long way from our school on Stadstimmertuinen. That afternoon I nearly fell asleep at my desk. Fortunately, people automatically offer you something to drink. The dental assistant is really kind.

3   The only mode of transportation left to us is the ferry. The ferryman at Josef Israëlkade took us across when we asked him to. It's not the fault of the Dutch that we Jews are having such a bad time.

everyone hates jews

4   I wish I didn't have to go to school. My bike was stolen during Easter vacation, and Father gave Mother's bike to some Christian friends for safekeeping. Thank goodness summer vacation is almost here; one more week and our torment will be over. *accepting their mistreatment*

5   Something unexpected happened yesterday morning. As I was passing the bicycle racks, I heard my name being called. I turned around and there was the nice boy I'd met the evening before at my friend Wilma's. He's Wilma's second cousin. I used to think Wilma was nice, which she is, but all she ever talks about is boys, and that gets to be a bore. He came toward me, somewhat shyly, and introduced himself as Hello Silberberg. I was a little surprised and wasn't sure what he wanted, but it didn't take me long to find out. He asked if I would allow him to accompany me to school. "As long as you're headed that way, I'll go with you," I said. And so we walked together. Hello is sixteen and good at telling all kinds of funny stories. *his name is Hello?*

6   He was waiting for me again this morning, and I expect he will be from now on.

7   Anne

WEDNESDAY, JULY 8, 1942

8   Dearest Kitty,

jews struggle w survival

9   It seems like years since Sunday morning. So much has happened it's as if the whole world had suddenly turned upside down. But as you can see, Kitty, I'm still alive, and that's the main thing, Father says. I'm alive all right, but don't ask where or how. You probably don't understand a word I'm saying today, so I'll begin by telling you what happened Sunday afternoon.

10   At three o'clock (Hello had left but was supposed to come back later), the doorbell rang. I didn't hear it, since I was out on the balcony, lazily reading in the sun. A little while later Margot appeared in the kitchen doorway looking very **agitated.** "Father has received a call-up notice from the SS," she whispered. "Mother has gone to see Mr. van Daan." (Mr. van Daan is Father's business partner and a good friend.)

11   I was stunned. A call-up: everyone knows what that means. Visions of concentration camps and lonely cells raced through my head. How could we let Father go to such a fate? "Of course he's not going," declared Margot as we waited for Mother in the living room. "Mother's gone to Mr. van Daan to ask whether we can move to our hiding place tomorrow. The van Daans are going with us. There will be seven of us altogether." Silence. We couldn't speak. The thought of Father off visiting someone in the Jewish Hospital and completely unaware of what was happening, the long wait for Mother, the heat, the suspense—all this reduced us to silence.

hello knows where she lives

12   Suddenly the doorbell rang again. "That's Hello," I said.

13   "Don't open the door!" exclaimed Margot to stop me. But it wasn't necessary, since we heard Mother and Mr. van Daan downstairs talking to Hello, and then the two of them came inside and shut the door behind them. Every time the bell rang, either Margot or I had to tiptoe downstairs to see if it was Father, *scared of mr vandaan* and we didn't let anyone else in. Margot and I were sent from the room, as Mr. van Daan wanted to talk to Mother alone.

14   When she and I were sitting in our bedroom, Margot told me that the call-up was not for Father, but for her. At this second shock, I began to cry. Margot is *is this for all girls or just jewish girls?* sixteen—apparently they want to send girls her age away on their own. But thank goodness she won't be going; Mother had said so herself, which must be what Father had meant when he talked to me about our going into hiding. Hiding . . . where would we hide? In the city? In the country? In a

jews are at risk to warm

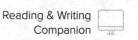

NOTES

shack? When, where, how . . . ? These were questions I wasn't allowed to ask, but they still kept running through my mind.

15 Margot and I started packing our most important belongings into a schoolbag. The first thing I stuck in was this diary, and then curlers, handkerchiefs, schoolbooks, a comb and some old letters. **Preoccupied** by the thought of going into hiding, I stuck the craziest things in the bag, but I'm not sorry. Memories mean more to me than dresses. ...

limited packing space

16 Yours, Anne

SATURDAY, JULY 11, 1942

17 Dearest Kitty,

18 Father, Mother, and Margot still can't get used to the chiming of the Westertoren clock, which tells us the time every quarter of an hour. Not me, I liked it from the start; it sounds so reassuring, especially at night. You no doubt want to hear what I think of being in hiding. Well, all I can say is that I don't really know yet. I don't think I'll ever feel at home in this house, but that doesn't mean I hate it. It's more like being on vacation in some strange pension. Kind of an odd way to look at life in hiding, but that's how things are. The Annex is an ideal place to hide in. It may be damp and **lopsided,** but there's probably not a more comfortable hiding place in all of Amsterdam. No, in all of Holland.

they're grateful for the worst things

19 Up to now our bedroom, with its blank walls, was very bare. Thanks to Father—who brought my entire postcard and movie-star collection here beforehand—and to a brush and a pot of glue, I was able to plaster the wall with pictures. It looks much more cheerful. When the Van Daans arrive, we"ll be able to build cupboards and other odds and ends out of the wood piled in the attic.

bad conditions

20 Margot and Mother have recovered somewhat. Yesterday Mother felt well enough to cook split-pea soup for the first time, but then she was downstairs talking and forgot all about it. The beans were scorched black, and no amount of scraping could get them out of the pan.

21 Last night the four of us went down to the private office and listened to England on the radio. I was so scared someone might hear it that I literally begged Father to take me back upstairs. Mother understood my **anxiety** and went with me. Whatever we do, we're very afraid the neighbors might hear or see us...

22 Yours, Anne

Excerpted from *Anne Frank: The Diary of a Young Girl* by Anne Frank, published by Doubleday.

THINK QUESTIONS
CA-CCSS: CA.RI.8.1, CA.L.8.4a, CA.L.8.4c, CA.SL.8.1a, CA.SL.8.1b, CA.SL.8.1c, CA.SL.8.1d

1. According to the text, what was one way Jews were discriminated against during the Nazi occupation of Amsterdam in the early 1940s? Cite details from the text to support your response.

2. What event takes place in the second entry of Anne Frank's diary? How does this event affect Anne's family? Cite details from the text to explain what takes place.

3. What does Anne pack to bring to the hiding place? Why does she pack these particular items? After she arrives, what does she do to make the hiding place feel more like home? Cite details from the text in your response.

4. Use context to determine the meaning of the word **agitated** as it is used within the text. Write your definition of *agitated*.

5. Look up the definition and part of speech of **lopsided** in a dictionary. Write the definition and part of speech that you found. Then rewrite the sentence in paragraph 18 in which *lopsided* appears, replacing this term with a synonym.

Please note that excerpts and passages in the StudySync® library and this workbook are intended as touchstones to generate interest in an author's work. The excerpts and passages do not substitute for the reading of entire texts, and StudySync® strongly recommends that students seek out and purchase the whole literary or informational work in order to experience it as the author intended. Links to online resellers are available in our digital library. In addition, complete works may be ordered through an authorized reseller by filling out and returning to StudySync® the order form enclosed in this workbook.

Reading & Writing Companion

13

CLOSE READ
CA-CCSS: CA.RI.8.1, CA.RI.8.2, CA.RI.8.3, CA.W.8.3b, CA.W.8.4, CA.W.8.5, CA.W.8.6, CA.W.8.10

Reread the excerpt from *Anne Frank: The Diary of a Young Girl.* As you reread, complete the Focus Questions below. Then use your answers and annotations from the questions to help you complete the Writing Prompt.

 FOCUS QUESTIONS

1. In this excerpt of the diary, readers learn how Anne Frank responded to the frightening circumstances she faced as a Jewish girl during the Holocaust. What do her diary entries suggest about the kind of person she was? Highlight details that reveal Anne's character, and make annotations to explain your ideas.

2. What is the central or main idea of the first entry of this excerpt? How does paragraph 4 support the main idea? Highlight textual details. Make annotations to write the main idea and to explain how the details support it.

3. What is the central or main idea of the second entry of this excerpt? Highlight details, especially in paragraph 10, that support the main idea. Make annotations to write the main idea and to explain how the details support it.

4. What does Anne Frank describe in the third entry of this excerpt? Highlight Anne's details about her mother and sister in the last two paragraphs. What do the details reveal about them and the situation? Make annotations to explain your ideas.

5. Highlight the dates in each of the diary entries in this excerpt. How do Anne's circumstances change between each entry? Make annotations to summarize the changes. Highlight details that will help you write your summary.

WRITING PROMPT

If Kitty were a person instead of a diary, Anne Frank might expect to receive a response. How might a friend respond to Anne in her time of crisis? Suppose you are Anne's friend and that the entries from her diary are letters to you. Choose one of the three entries and write a letter to Anne in response. Be sure to include an appropriate day, date, greeting, and signature. Refer to details from her letter, including Anne's central idea, in your response. If you wish, you may also include fictional details as if you lived during that time. Use narrative techniques, such as pacing, description, and reflection, to develop the experiences and events you describe in your letters.

THE DIARY OF ANNE FRANK: A PLAY

DRAMA
Frances Goodrich and
Albert Hackett
1955

INTRODUCTION

studysync tv

rances Goodrich and Albert Hackett's drama based on Anne Frank's *The Diary of Young Girl* provides a first-hand account of the persecution of the Jewish people by the Nazis during World War II. The excerpt below comes from early in the play, with Miep, one of the family's confidants, showing Mr. Frank the secret rooms that hid them.

"Yesterday Father told me we were going into hiding."

 FIRST READ

Act I, Scene 1

1   *The curtain rises on an empty stage. It is late afternoon November, 1945.*

2   *The rooms are dusty, the curtains in rags. Chairs and tables are overturned.*

3   *The door at the foot of the small stairwell swings open.* MR. FRANK *comes up the steps into view. He is a gentle,* **cultured** *European in his middle years. There is still a trace of a German accent in his speech.*

4   *He stands looking slowly around, making a supreme effort at self-control. He is weak, ill. His clothes are* **threadbare.**

5   *After a second he drops his* **rucksack** *on the couch and moves slowly about. He opens the door to one of the smaller rooms, and then abruptly closes it again, turning away. He goes to the window at the back, looking off at the Westertoren as its carillon strikes the hour of six, then he moves restlessly on.*

6   *From the street below, we hear the sound of a barrel organ and children's voices at play. There is a many-colored scarf hanging from a nail.* MR. FRANK *takes it, putting it around his neck. As he starts back for his rucksack, his eye is caught by something lying on the floor. It is a woman's white glove. He holds it in his hand and suddenly all of his self-control is gone. He breaks down, crying.*

7   *We hear footsteps on the stairs.* MIEP GIES *comes up, looking for* MR. FRANK. MIEP *is a Dutch girl of about twenty-two. She wears a coat and hat, ready to go home. She is pregnant. Her attitude toward* MR. FRANK *is protective, compassionate.*

8   MIEP: Are you all right, Mr. Frank?

9   MR. FRANK [*quickly controlling himself*]: Yes, Miep, yes.

10 MIEP: Everyone in the office has gone home... It's after six. [*then pleading*] Don't stay up here, Mr. Frank. What's the use of torturing yourself like this?

11 MR. FRANK: I've come to say good-bye... I'm leaving here, Miep.

12 MIEP: What do you mean? Where are you going? Where?

13 MR. FRANK: I don't know yet. I haven't decided.

14 MIEP: Mr. Frank, you can't leave here! This is your home! Amsterdam is your home. Your business is here, waiting for you... You're needed here... Now that the war is over, there are things that...

15 MR. FRANK: I can't stay in Amsterdam, Miep. It has too many memories for me. Everywhere there's something... the house we lived in... the school... that street organ playing out there... I'm not the person you used to know, Miep. I'm a bitter old man. [*breaking off*] Forgive me, I shouldn't speak to you like this... after all that you did for us... the suffering...

16 MIEP: No. No. It wasn't suffering. You can't say we suffered. [*As she speaks, she straightens a chair which is overturned.*]

17 MR. FRANK: I know what you went through, you and Mr. Kraler. I'll remember it as long as I live. [*He gives one last look around.*] Come, Miep. [*He starts for the steps, then remembers his rucksack, going back to get it.*]

18 MIEP [*hurrying up to a cupboard*]: Mr. Frank, did you see? There are some of your papers here. [*She brings a bundle of papers to him.*] We found them in a heap of rubbish on the floor after... after you left.

19 MR. FRANK: Burn them. [*He opens his rucksack to put the glove in it.*]

20 MIEP: But, Mr. Frank, there are letters, notes...

21 MR. FRANK: Burn them. All of them.

22 MIEP: Burn this? [*She hands him a paperbound notebook.*]

23 MR FRANK [*quietly*]: Anne's diary. [*He opens the diary and begins to read.*] "Monday, the sixth of July, nineteen forty-two." [*to* MIEP] Nineteen forty-two. Is it possible, Miep? ... Only three years ago. [*As he continues his reading, he sits down on the couch.*] "Dear Diary, since you and I are going to be great friends, I will start by telling you about myself. My name is Anne Frank. I am thirteen years old. I was born in Germany the twelfth of June, nineteen twenty-nine. As my family is Jewish, we **emigrated** to Holland when Hitler came to power."

24   [*As* MR. FRANK *reads, another voice joins his, as if coming from the air. It is* ANNE'S VOICE.]

25   MR. FRANK and ANNE: "My father started a business, importing spice and herbs. Things went well for us until nineteen forty. Then the war came, and the Dutch **capitulation,** followed by the arrival of the Germans. Then things got very bad for the Jews."

26   [MR. FRANK'S VOICE *dies out.* ANNE'S VOICE *continues alone. The lights dim slowly to darkness. The curtain falls on the scene.*]

27   ANNE'S VOICE: You could not do this and you could not do that. They forced Father out of his business. We had to wear yellow stars. I had to turn in my bike. I couldn't go to a Dutch school any more. I couldn't go to the movies, or ride in an automobile or even on a streetcar, and a million other things. But somehow we children still managed to have fun. Yesterday Father told me we were going into hiding. Where, he wouldn't say. At five o'clock this morning Mother woke me and told me to hurry and get dressed. I was to put on as many clothes as I could. It would look too suspicious if we walked along carrying suitcases. It wasn't until we were on our way that I learned where we were going. Our hiding place was to be upstairs in the building where Father used to have his business. Three other people were coming in with us—the Van Daans and their son Peter. Father knew the Van Daans but we had never met them.

28   [*During the last lines the curtain rises on the scene. The lights dim on.* ANNE'S VOICE *fades out.*]

Excerpted from *The Diary of Anne Frank: A Play* by Frances Goodrich and Albert Hackett, published by Nelson Thornes Ltd.

THINK QUESTIONS CA-CCSS: CA.RL.8.1, CA.L.8.4a, CA.SL.8.1b, CA.SL.8.1c, CA.SL.8.1d

1. Why does Mr. Frank break down crying, as described in the stage direction that begins this passage? Use evidence from the text and your prior knowledge of Mr. Frank's history to support your answer.

2. Why is Mr. Frank grateful to Miep? Use evidence from the text and your prior knowledge of Mr. Frank's history to support your answer.

3. Did Anne Frank begin keeping a diary before or after she and her family went into hiding? Support your answer with textual evidence.

4. Use context to determine the meaning of the word **rucksack** as it is used in the passage. Write your definition of *rucksack* and tell how you found it.

5. Use context to determine the meaning of the word **emigrated** as it is used in the passage. Write your definition of *emigrated* and tell how you found it.

Please note that excerpts and passages in the StudySync® library and this workbook are intended as touchstones to generate interest in an author's work. The excerpts and passages do not substitute for the reading of entire texts, and StudySync® strongly recommends that students seek out and purchase the whole literary or informational work in order to experience it as the author intended. Links to online resellers are available in our digital library. In addition, complete works may be ordered through an authorized reseller by filling out and returning to StudySync® the order form enclosed in this workbook.

Reading & Writing Companion **19**

CLOSE READ

CA-CCSS: CA.RL.8.1, CA.RL.8.2, CA.RL.8.3, CA.RL.8.7, CA.W.8.4, CA.W.8.5, CA.W.8.6, CA.W.8.10

Reread the excerpt from the drama *The Diary of a Young Girl: A Play.* As you reread, complete the Focus Questions below. Then use your answers and annotations from the questions to help you complete the Writing Prompt.

 FOCUS QUESTIONS

1. How to live with the pain of memory is one of the questions, and themes, in *The Diary of Anne Frank: A Play.* How is this theme revealed in the conflict Mr. Frank feels within himself when he returns to the attic rooms? Support your answer with evidence from the text.

2. The stage directions that open the play reveal that the rooms are dusty, the curtains are in rags, and tables and chairs are overturned. Mr. Frank walks onstage and finds a scarf and a woman's white glove. In the film, Mr. Frank arrives at the annex and stands on the street in front of the building. The viewer sees him through a window in the attic room as he looks up at the building. Later, as he walks through the dark rooms, Mr. Frank's face is mostly hidden, until he becomes a black silhouette. How does the camera make the attic setting seem almost like another character in the film? Support your answer with evidence from the film.

3. The stage directions in the play reveal a great deal about the characters, but much information about them is also revealed through the dialogue. Explain how the author uses dialogue to help readers understand the characters of Miep and Mr. Frank in this excerpt. Highlight dialogue that reveals information about each character, and make annotations to explain what you can infer about the characters from what they say.

4. Highlight the stage directions in the play that introduce and describe Anne. The stage directions indicate that as Mr. Frank reads from Anne's diary, "another voice joins his, as if coming from the air." Why do you think Anne is introduced in this way? Support your answer with evidence from the text.

5. What does Anne's monologue at the end of the excerpt, an entry from her diary, reveal about the difficulties the Frank family will face in the future? Highlight textual evidence and make annotations to explain your ideas.

WRITING PROMPT

How does political or national conflict influence individual families? How does *The Diary of Anne Frank: A Play* explore this theme? What elements of the play help you understand this influence? Support your answer with text evidence from the selection.

THE BOY IN THE STRIPED PAJAMAS: A FABLE

FICTION
John Boyne
2006

INTRODUCTION

Written by Irish author John Boyne, *The Boy in the Striped Pajamas* has become a worldwide bestseller and has won numerous book awards. The novel tells the story of the friendship between two young boys—Bruno, the son of a high-ranking SS officer, and Shmuel, a Jewish boy who is a prisoner at Auschwitz concentration camp (called Out-With in the book). Though immensely popular, the book has not been without criticism. While many have praised it as a powerful tale of friendship amidst the horrors of war, others have criticized the book for trivializing the Holocaust.

"The boy stared at the food in his hand for a moment and then looked up at Bruno..."

 FIRST READ

Excerpt from Chapter Fifteen: Something He Shouldn't Have Done

1   Bruno went into the kitchen and got the biggest surprise of his life. There, sitting at the table, a long way from the other side of the fence, was Shmuel. Bruno could barely believe his eyes.

2   "Shmuel!" he said. "What are you doing here?"

3   Shmuel looked up and his terrified face broke into a broad smile when he saw his friend standing there. "Bruno!" he said.

4   "What are you doing here?" repeated Bruno, for although he still didn't quite understand what took place on the other side of the fence, there was something about the people from there that made him think they shouldn't be here in his house.

5   "He brought me," said Shmuel.

6   "He?" asked Bruno. "You don't mean Lieutenant Kotler?"

7   "Yes. He said there was a job for me to do here."

8   And when Bruno looked down he saw sixty-four small glasses, the ones Mother used when she was having one of her medicinal sherries, sitting on the kitchen table, and beside them a bowl of warm soapy water and lots of paper napkins.

9   "What on earth are you doing?" asked Bruno.

10 "They asked me to polish the glasses," said Shmuel. "They said they needed someone with tiny fingers."

11   As if to prove something that Bruno already knew, he held his hand out and Bruno couldn't help but notice that it was like the hand of the pretend skeleton that Herr Liszt had brought with him one day when they were studying human **anatomy.**

12   "I'd never noticed before," he said in a **disbelieving** voice, almost to himself.

13   "Never noticed what?" said Shmuel.

14   In reply, Bruno held his own hand out so that the tips of their middle fingers were almost touching. "Our hands," he said. "They're so different. Look!"

15   The two boys looked down at the same time and the difference was easy to see. Although Bruno was small for his age, and certainly not fat, his hand appeared healthy and full of life. The veins weren't visible through the skin, the fingers weren't little more than dying twigs. Shmuel's hand, however, told a very different story.

16   "How did it get like that?" he asked.

17   "I don't know," said Shmuel. "It used to look more like yours, but I didn't notice it changing. Everyone on my side of the fence looks like this now."

18   Bruno frowned. He thought about the people in their striped pajamas and wondered what was going on at Out-With and whether it wasn't a very bad idea if it made people look so unhealthy. None of it made any sense to him. Not wanting to look at Shmuel's hand any longer, Bruno turned round and opened the refrigerator, **rooting** about inside it for something to eat. There was half a stuffed chicken left over from lunch time, and Bruno's eyes sparkled in delight for there were very few things in life that he enjoyed more than cold chicken with **sage** and onion stuffing. He took a knife from the drawer and cut himself a few healthy slices and coated them with the stuffing before turning back to his friend.

19   "I'm very glad you're here," he said, speaking with his mouth full. "If only you didn't have to polish the glasses, I could show you my room."

20   "He told me not to move from this seat or there'd be trouble."

21   "I wouldn't mind him," said Bruno, trying to sound braver than he really was. "This isn't his house, it's mine, and when Father's away I'm in charge. Can you believe he's never even read *Treasure Island*?"

22   Shmuel looked as if he wasn't really listening; instead his eyes were focused on the slices of chicken and stuffing that Bruno was throwing casually into his

mouth. After a moment Bruno realized what he was looking at and immediately felt guilty.

23 "I'm sorry Shmuel," he said quickly. "I should have given you some chicken too. Are you hungry?"

24 "That's a question you never have to ask me," said Shmuel who, although he had never met Gretel in his life, knew something about sarcasm too.

25 "Wait there, I'll cut some off for you," said Bruno, opening the fridge and cutting another three healthy slices.

26 "No, if he comes back—" said Shmuel, shaking his head quickly and looking back and forth towards the door.

27 "If who comes back? You don't mean Lieutenant Kotler?"

28 "I'm just supposed to be cleaning the glasses," he said, looking at the bowl of water in front of him in despair and then looking back at the slices of chicken that Bruno held out to him.

29 "He's not going to mind," said Bruno, who was confused by how anxious Shmuel seemed. "It's only food."

30 "I can't," said Shmuel, shaking his head and looking as if he was going to cry. "He'll come back, I know he will," he continued, his sentences running quickly together. "I should have eaten them when you offered them, now it's too late, if I take them he'll come in and—"

31 "Shmuel! Here!" said Bruno, stepping forward and putting the slices in his friend's hand. "Just eat them. There's lots left for our tea—you don't have to worry about that."

32 The boy stared at the food in his hand for a moment and then looked up at Bruno with wide and grateful but terrified eyes. He threw one more glance in the direction of the door and then seemed to make a decision, because he thrust all three slices into his mouth in one go and gobbled them down in twenty seconds flat.

33 "Well, you don't have to eat them so quickly," said Bruno. "You'll make yourself sick."

34 "I don't care," said Shmuel, giving a faint smile. "Thank you, Bruno."

35 Bruno smiled back and he was about to offer him some more food, but just at that moment Lieutenant Kotler reappeared in the kitchen and stopped when he saw the two boys talking. Bruno stared at him, feeling the atmosphere

Reading & Writing Companion

grow heavy, sensing Shmuel's shoulders sinking down as he reached for another glass and began polishing. Ignoring Bruno, Lieutenant Kotler marched over to Shmuel and glared at him.

36 "What are you doing?" he shouted. "Didn't I tell you to polish these glasses?"

37 Shmuel nodded his head quickly and started to tremble a little as he picked up another napkin and dipped it in the water.

38 "Who told you that you were allowed to talk in this house?" continued Kotler. "Do you dare to disobey me?"

39 "No, sir," said Shmuel quietly. "I'm sorry, sir."

40 He looked up at Lieutenant Kotler, who frowned, leaning forward slightly and tilting his head as he examined the boy's face. "Have you been eating?" he asked him in a quiet voice, as if he could scarcely believe it himself.

41 Shmuel shook his head.

42 "You *have* been eating," insisted Lieutenant Kotler. "Did you steal something from that fridge?"

43 Shmuel opened his mouth and closed it. He opened it again and tried to find words, but there were none. He looked towards Bruno, his eyes pleading for help.

44 "Answer me!" shouted Lieutenant Kotler. "Did you steal something from that fridge?"

45 "No, sir. He gave it to me," said Shmuel, tears **welling** up in his eyes as he threw a sideways glance at Bruno. "He's my friend," he added.

46 "Your...?" began Lieutenant Kotler, looking across at Bruno in confusion. He hesitated. "What do you mean he's your friend?" he asked. "Do you know this boy, Bruno?"

47 Bruno's mouth dropped open and he tried to remember the way you used your mouth if you wanted to say the word "yes". He'd never seen anyone look so terrified as Shmuel did at that moment and he wanted to say the right thing to make things better, but then he realized that he couldn't; because he was feeling just as terrified himself.

Excerpted from *The Boy in the Striped Pajamas: A Fable* by John Boyne, published by David Fickling Books.

Please note that excerpts and passages in the StudySync® library and this workbook are intended as touchstones to generate interest in an author's work. The excerpts and passages do not substitute for the reading of entire texts, and StudySync® strongly recommends that students seek out and purchase the whole literary or informational work in order to experience it as the author intended. Links to online resellers are available in our digital library. In addition, complete works may be ordered through an authorized reseller by filling out and returning to StudySync® the order form enclosed in this workbook.

Reading & Writing Companion   25

THINK QUESTIONS CA-CCSS: CA.RL.8.1, CA.RL.8.4, CA.L.8.4a, CA.L.8.4b

1. Before finding Shmuel in his house, Bruno had never noticed how thin Shmuel's fingers were, like "dying twigs." Why do Shmuel's and Bruno's hands look so different? Use evidence from the text to support your answer.

2. Why isn't Bruno afraid of Lieutenant Kotler at first? Use evidence from the text to support your response.

3. What additional evidence does the author provide that suggests Bruno has no idea what really goes on at "Out-With" as he calls it?

4. Use context to determine the meaning of the word **rooting** as it is used in *The Boy in the Striped Pajamas*. Write your definition of *rooting* and tell how you found it.

5. Remembering that the Latin prefix *dis-* can mean "not," use the context clues provided in the passage to determine the meaning of **disbelieving.** Write your definition of *disbelieving* and tell how you got it.

CLOSE READ   CA-CCSS: CA.RL.8.1, CA.RL.8.2, CA.RL.8.3, CA.RL.8.6, CA.W.8.2

Reread the excerpt from *The Boy in the Striped Pajamas: A Fable.* As you reread, complete the Focus Questions below. Then use your answers and annotations from the questions to help you complete the Writing Prompt.

FOCUS QUESTIONS

1. Explain how the author uses the first several paragraphs to establish the point of view in the story. Highlight evidence from the text and make annotations to explain your choices.

2. Reread paragraphs 18 and 19 that begin with the words "Bruno frowned" and end with ".... I could show you my room." What do Bruno's thoughts, actions, and dialogue reveal about his character?

3. Reread paragraphs 20 through 30 beginning with "He told me not to move" and ending with "...if I take them he'll come in and—." What can you infer about Shmuel's character from the dialogue in these paragraphs?

4. In the 18th paragraph that begins with "Bruno frowned," the term "Out-With" is mentioned. Who or what is "Out-With"? How is Lieutenant Kotler a symbol for this larger, although unseen, antagonist? Use evidence from the text to support your response.

5. In the last eight paragraphs of the story, all three characters have conflicts. Discuss these conflicts with a focus on the Essential Question for this unit: "What does our response to conflict say about us?" Use evidence from the text to support your response.

WRITING PROMPT

How can point of view and character shape the overall theme of a text? Identify the theme of *The Boy in the Striped Pajamas: A Fable* and discuss how character and point of view contribute to the theme. Include textual evidence to support your writing.

Please note that excerpts and passages in the StudySync® library and this workbook are intended as touchstones to generate interest in an author's work. The excerpts and passages do not substitute for the reading of entire texts, and StudySync® strongly recommends that students seek out and purchase the whole literary or informational work in order to experience it as the author intended. Links to online resellers are available in our digital library. In addition, complete works may be ordered through an authorized reseller by filling out and returning to StudySync® the order form enclosed in this workbook.

Reading & Writing
Companion   27

TEACHING
HISTORY
THROUGH
FICTION

NON-FICTION
2015

INTRODUCTION

Teaching history through fiction can capture the imaginations of young readers and bring history alive. But using historical fiction to teach history is not without risks. Authors of historical fiction are not always primarily concerned with teaching history. Such is the case with John Boyne, author of *The Boy in the Striped Pajamas*. Boyne subtitled his book "A Fable" to alert readers to the fact that he had altered some realities of the Holocaust. But is that enough? The writers in these two articles explore whether Boyne's desire to explore the moral issues of the Holocaust from the perspective of children outweighs the dangers of distorting the historical realities of this dark time in history.

"Fiction can make history matter—make it irresistible—to young readers."

FIRST READ

Teaching History Through Fiction: Valuable or Dangerous?

Point: There is Value in Teaching History Through Fiction

1   Every history teacher knows that making students believe that history is relevant to their lives is Challenge Number 1. The question is, how can this difficult feat be accomplished? One answer lies in a source we might least expect: fiction. As Valerie Tripp points out in her blog entry on the teachinghistory.org website, "Fiction can make history matter—make it irresistible—to young readers" (Tripp). This effect is achieved by John Boyne's *The Boy in the Striped Pajamas.* By approaching the Holocaust through the eyes of two nine-year-old boys, the book provides a unique perspective on this dark and horrible chapter in history. Fiction, including stories, novels, and films, is a great way to teach people about history, and John Boyne's *The Boy in the Striped Pajamas* is an excellent example.

2   Reviewers and readers alike praise the book. Boyne notes on his website that the novel has sold more than six million copies worldwide. In addition to reaching the top of the *New York Times* Best Seller list, *The Boy in the Striped Pajamas* has won many awards. Not surprisingly, it was made into a movie in 2008 (Boyne). Reviewers have offered equally high praise for the movie. Film critic Peter Rainer notes in his online movie review for the *Christian Science Monitor,* "The great conundrum of the Holocaust is that it was perpetrated by human beings, not monsters. Few movies have rendered this puzzle so powerfully" (Rainer, "Review: *The Boy in the Striped Pajamas*"). It is interesting to note that Rainer has also reviewed Richard Linklater's *Boyhood. Boyhood* is another child-centered movie.

3   Critics of the novel and movie argue that both are historically inaccurate. The premise of the story is the friendship between Bruno, the son of the German commandant at Auschwitz, and Shmuel, a Jewish boy imprisoned in the

Please note that excerpts and passages in the StudySync® library and this workbook are intended as touchstones to generate interest in an author's work. The excerpts and passages do not substitute for the reading of entire texts, and StudySync® strongly recommends that students seek out and purchase the whole literary or informational work in order to experience it as the author intended. Links to online resellers are available in our digital library. In addition, complete works may be ordered through an authorized reseller by filling out and returning to StudySync® the order form enclosed in this workbook.

Reading & Writing Companion   **29**

concentration camp. Over the course of a year, the boys' friendship grows as they meet and talk for hours at the camp's fence. Innocent Bruno does not understand why his friend cannot leave the camp to play or why Shmuel must wear the striped pajamas. Critics, like David Cesarani, argue that Bruno's innocence is unrealistic. A nine-year-old boy in wartime Germany would clearly understand the purpose of the camp and why Shmuel was there. This would be particularly true for the son of a high-ranking Nazi (Cesarani). That may be true. But these critics are missing the point. As Claudia Moscovici notes in her literature blog, the subtitle clearly indicates that *The Boy in the Striped Pajamas* is a fable. "By its own admission," Moscovici argues, "this novel doesn't propose to offer a realistic historical account of the Holocaust" (Moscovici). Fables are not history. Fables are designed to explore moral lessons. Both the novel and movie do just that through their touching and thought-provoking exploration of the moral issues surrounding the Holocaust.

4   Reviewer Kathryn Hughes, writing in the online edition of the *Guardian* newspaper, sums up the value of *The Boy in the Striped Pajamas.* She writes, "For the older reader, of course, Bruno's innocence comes to stand for the willful refusal of all adult Germans to see what was going on under their noses in the first half of the 1940s." For younger readers, she argues, the story's slow release of details "becomes an education in real time of the horrors of 'Out-With,' known to the grown-ups as Auschwitz" (Hughes). This is exactly what we expect of the fiction we use to teach history.

5   As Joanne Brown notes in her article on writing historical fiction for young adults, "Any writer who tells a story set in the past must negotiate the fine line between history and fiction, between readers' contemporary sensibilities and historical accuracy." Admittedly, some of the literary devices in *The Boy in the Striped Pajamas* might require readers familiar with the Holocaust to accept some historical inaccuracy (Brown). For example, as Cesarani points out, the fences of the camps "were heavily guarded and frequently electrified" (Cesarani). Thus it is doubtful that Bruno and Shmuel could sit for hours and talk. But in the end, this is not important. Boyne's main purpose in writing this novel was not to teach young readers facts about the Holocaust. His main goal was to present a story that would move them to want to learn more about the subject (Boyne).

6   The goal of good fiction should be to move people. It should move them to laugh, to cry, to care, to think—or else why should they bother reading it? History too should move people—or else how will they learn from it? By exploring the moral issues of the Holocaust through the eyes of two innocent young boys, *The Boy in the Striped Pajamas* accomplishes what should be important aims of both fiction and history: it moves people to care and to think. Thus, the story is an excellent example of how to teach history through fiction.

Counterpoint: There is Danger in Fictionalizing History

7   Teaching history through the use of fiction, including stories, novels, and films, is often misleading and can be dangerous, and John Boyne's *The Boy in the Striped Pajamas* shows why. By manipulating the historical realities of the Holocaust for the sake of a good story, Boyne runs the risk of giving readers a distorted view of the Holocaust.

8   No one would consider Valerie Tripp an opponent of using fiction to teach history. On the teachinghistory.org website, Tripp notes that "fiction can make history matter—make it irresistible—to young readers" (Tripp, "Vitamins in Chocolate Cake"). Yet Tripp, an author of youth fiction herself, also knows the dangers. She offers this warning to teachers: "When choosing historical fiction to use in the classroom as a way to interest students in history, I'd say: First, do no harm. That is, before it is used in a history classroom, historical fiction should be checked for bias, for anachronistic voice and views, and for shying away from honest presentation of the period. What is not said is as misleading as what is said!" (Tripp, "Neither Spinach Nor Potato Chip").

9   Judged according to Tripp's criteria, teachers should use *The Boy in the Striped Pajamas* with caution. Boyne's bias rests not in his personal beliefs about the Holocaust, but in his view of storytelling. In an interview with Alexis Burling on Teenreads.com, Boyne explains how he approached the story:

10   Considering the serious subject matter of this novel and the fact that I would be taking certain aspects of concentration camp history and changing them slightly in order to serve the story, I felt it was important not to pretend that a story like this was fully based in reality (which was also the reason why I chose never to use the word "Auschwitz" in the novel). My understanding of the term "fable" is a piece of fiction that contains a moral. I hope that the moral at the center of THE BOY IN THE STRIPED PAJAMAS is self-evident to readers. (Burling)

11 Personally, I don't like fables. But that aside, the problem with Boyne's premise is that writing a fable does not release him from an author's obligation not to distort history. This is particularly true when dealing with an event as serious as the Holocaust. The danger of "serving the story" over serving the facts is that young readers will not know enough Holocaust history to understand what has been changed. As critic David Cesarani notes, "Except for a few peculiar cases there were no Jewish children in the extermination camps: they were gassed on arrival" (Cesarani). Thus the very premise of the story is, in Cesarani's words, "utterly implausible." In his scathing review of the book, Cesarani explains why the implausibility matters: "Should this matter if the book is a 'fable' which is presumably intended by its author to warn against the evils of prejudice? Yes. Because there are people at large who contest

whether the systematic mass murder of the Jews occurred" (Cesarani). This is a serious charge, especially given that, according to Boyne's website, the book has sold more than six million copies worldwide and has been made into a movie (Boyne).

12   The critics of the book and the 2008 movie are many. One of their complaints is Boyne's use of clever word devices to avoid addressing the real facts of the Holocaust. Young Bruno mishears "Auschwitz" as "Out-With" and "the Führer" as "the Fury." As Cesarani points out, "Any normal German nine-year-old would have been able to pronounce Führer and Auschwitz correctly." Also, Bruno's word choices are culturally misplaced. As reviewer A. O. Scott notes, "There is something illogical about them, since Bruno's native language is presumably German in which the portentous puns would make no sense, not English, in which they do" (Scott).

13   More serious complaints involve what Tripp calls "shying away from honest presentation of the period." Most notably, even if there had been a lot of Jewish children at Auschwitz, the idea that the commandant's son and one of those children would meet repeatedly is beyond belief. As critics note, the two boys would not have had the opportunity. Guards patrolled the fences and prisoners did not have the freedom to move about at will. Boyne's literary device hides the ugly truth of the concentration camps: constant roll calls, slave labor, forced marches, and guards with vicious dogs (Cesarani; Moscovici).

14   For these reasons, I believe that *The Boy in the Striped Pajamas* is a perfect example of why using fiction to teach history can be dangerous. Teachers are wise to keep Valerie Tripp's warning in mind when presenting the book: "What is not said is as misleading as what is said!"

THINK QUESTIONS CA-CCSS: CA.RI.8.1, CA.RI.8.4, CA.L.8.4a, CA.L.8.4b

1. The writer of the Point, "The Value of Teaching History Through Fiction," and the writer of the Counterpoint, "The Dangers of Fictionalizing History," share their views of using fiction to teach history. How do their ideas differ? Cite textual details to summarize the main points that each essay writer makes.

2. The Point writer cites Kathryn Hughes as a source to support her view. Summarize Hughes's view of the value of *The Boy in the Striped Pajamas*. How does what Hughes says help support the claim made in the Point essay? Support your answer with textual evidence and inferences.

3. One of the arguments the writer of the Counterpoint essays makes is that Boyne's clever wordplay is inappropriate. Identify what the wordplay is and the experts' arguments. How do the experts help the author support his claim? Support your answer with textual evidence.

4. Use context to determine the meaning of the word **conundrum** as it is used in the Point essay. Write your definition of *conundrum* and explain how you arrived at it.

5. Remembering that the Greek prefix *ana-* means "against," the Greek root *chron* means "time," and the suffix *-istic* means "characteristic of," use your knowledge of affixes and roots and the context clues in the Counterpoint essay to determine the meaning of **anachronistic.** Write your definition of *anachronistic* and explain how you arrived at it.

Please note that excerpts and passages in the StudySync® library and this workbook are intended as touchstones to generate interest in an author's work. The excerpts and passages do not substitute for the reading of entire texts, and StudySync® strongly recommends that students seek out and purchase the whole literary or informational work in order to experience it as the author intended. Links to online resellers are available in our digital library. In addition, complete works may be ordered through an authorized reseller by filling out and returning to StudySync® the order form enclosed in this workbook.

Reading & Writing Companion   **33**

CLOSE READ
CA-CCSS: CA.RI.8.1, CA.RI.8.2, CA.RI.8.5, CA.RI.8.8, CA.RI.8.9, CA.W.8.4, CA.W.8.5, CA.W.8.6, CA.W.8.9b, CA.W.8.10, CA.SL.8.3

Reread the text "Teaching History Through Fiction." As you reread, complete the Focus Questions below. Then use your answers and annotations from the questions to help you complete the Writing Prompt.

FOCUS QUESTIONS

1. Both writers provide bibliographies—lists of online sources they used to write their essays. As far as you can judge without actually consulting these links, are the sources reputable, and do they appear likely to provide accurate information? How does your analysis of the bibliography affect your opinion of the persuasiveness of each essay? Use specific details from the bibliographies and essays in your response.

2. Choose one example in either essay of weak, incomplete, or irrelevant evidence, and analyze what makes this evidence ineffective. How does the writer's choice to include this evidence affect your overall impression of the essay, and why? Use specific details and relevant textual evidence from the essay to support your answer.

3. Both writers base their arguments on *The Boy in the Striped Pajamas*. On the surface, this seems strange. How can a book be both a good example of using fiction to teach history and a good example of why using fiction to teach history can be dangerous? Cite evidence from both essays to explain how the writers structure their arguments to make this strategy work.

4. The two writers cite some of the same sources. Pick one of those sources and compare and contrast how the writers use the evidence in similar or different ways. Then evaluate whether one or both of the writers is twisting the evidence. Back up your ideas with text evidence.

5. Summarize the claims and key points of both essays. How effectively does each writer use evidence to support his or her position? What makes the evidence effective or ineffective? Which argument seems more convincing? Use specific details from both essays to support your answer.

WRITING PROMPT

Both essays focus on *The Boy in the Striped Pajamas* in discussing the role of fiction in teaching history. But the writers approach the book from different perspectives. Compare and contrast the perspectives. Which argument is more effective and persuasive? How might you suggest making it even stronger? Use textual evidence from both passages to support your response.

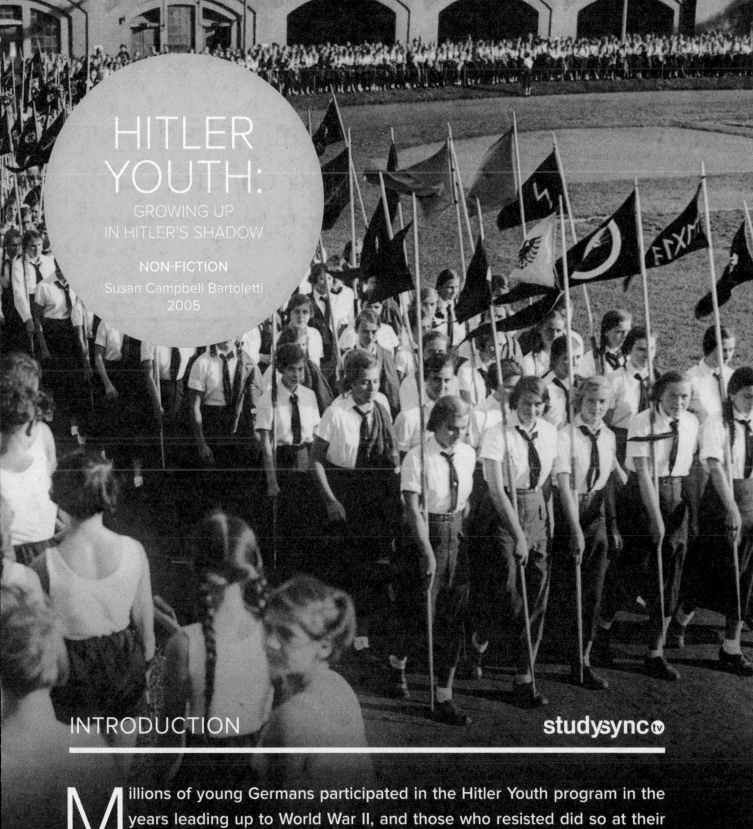

HITLER YOUTH:
GROWING UP IN HITLER'S SHADOW

NON-FICTION
Susan Campbell Bartoletti
2005

INTRODUCTION

Millions of young Germans participated in the Hitler Youth program in the years leading up to World War II, and those who resisted did so at their peril. Through diaries, letters, photographs, oral histories, and interviews, Susan Campbell Bartoletti's book illustrates what life was like for children growing up under Hitler. The excerpt below describes the Nazis' use of schools to further their goals. Sophie Scholl, a teenager discussed in the passage, was later beheaded for distributing anti-Nazi leaflets.

"For Hitler, education had one purpose: to mold children into good Nazis."

FIRST READ

Excerpt from Chapter Three: "Where One Burns Books" – A Nazi Education

1   At fourteen, Sophie Scholl moved from the Jungmädel to the older Bund Deutscher Mädel. Just as her sister Inge and brother Hans did, she believed that Hitler would help Germany achieve greatness, fortune, and prosperity.

2   Deeply sensitive, Sophie was a talented artist. She loved music, and, like many teenagers, she longed for individuality and independence. Although a German motto said, "German girls wear braids," dark-haired Sophie wore her hair short.

3   During high school, Sophie began to grow away from the National Socialistic ideas about race, religion, and duty. She was beginning to form her own political views, which she often wrote about in her diary and letters.

4   But to Sophie's dismay, her Nazi teachers did not tolerate disagreement or discussion of other viewpoints. Though Sophie knew the correct National Socialistic answer to every question, she soon found herself unwilling to give her teachers the answers they wanted but she felt were wrong.

↑ forming independence and firm beliefs

5   Sophie measured herself against high standards and believed others should do the same. "We all have this yardstick inside ourselves, but it just isn't sought enough. Maybe because it is the most difficult yardstick," she explained in a letter to her boyfriend, Fritz Hartnagel. Four years older than Sophie, Fritz was a young officer in the German army.   *↑ EW*

6   In school, Sophie felt **alienated** because she could not confide in a classmate or teacher. She longed to graduate and join her older brother, Hans, whom she adored, at the University of Munich, where she planned to study biology and philosophy.

NOTES

7 But for now, Sophie was stuck in high school, feeling frustrated and stifled. One day, she stopped raising her hand to be called upon. Her silence frustrated her teachers. The principal warned Sophie that she might not graduate if she didn't participate and show more enthusiasm for National Socialism. The threat worked: Worried now, Sophie **buckled** and studied hard to pass the Abitur, a difficult graduation test, in order to receive her diploma. Her diploma was her ticket to the university.

8 Later, Sophie would not buckle again on her political views: In another letter to Fritz, she wrote, "I don't like to think about it, but soon there is going to be nothing left but politics, and as long as it's so confused and evil, it's cowardly to turn away from it."

9 Sophie's frustration during high school stemmed from the Nazis' new **standardized** school curriculum. It was important to Adolf Hitler that all Germans shared the same outlook on the world. This was called *Weltanschauung,* or "worldview."

10 Although a poor student himself, Hitler had definite ideas about education. For Hitler, education had one purpose: to mold children into good Nazis. As soon as the Nazis came to power, they took control of the public schools, called National Schools. They threw out old textbooks and **implemented** new ones. They rewrote the curriculum from the top to bottom, so that it only taught Nazi-approved ideas.

11 Soon, the Nazi flag and Hitler's portrait hung in every classroom. "In the morning, we stood at attention, and there was the Nazi flag," said Karl Schnibbe. "We always had to start class with 'HeilHitler!' There was no more, 'Good morning, children.'"

12 The Nazis wanted to ensure that the teachers were politically reliable and supported the National Socialist Party and its principles. To accomplish this end, teachers were given a choice: Either join the National Socialist Teacher's Alliance and train the students in National Socialism or be dismissed.

13 The Hitler Youth enjoyed the power they had over teachers and other authority figures. Dressed in full uniform, entire Hitler Youth squads—as many as one hundred boys—showed up at classroom doors to **intimidate** teachers who did not espouse the Nazi worldview.

↑ students intimidating teacher and not the other way around??

14 In Munich, they broke up teachers' association meetings and even smashed out the apartment windows of a Latin teacher who had given out low grades. The police were called, but the Nazi Party wouldn't allow them to arrest the Hitler Youth. All the police could do was take down their names. Never before had students felt so much power over adults and school authority. But the

leader of the Hitler Youth, Baldur van Schirach, was unhappy about the unfavorable publicity, and he told the Hitler Youth to obey the law.

15   The Nazi Party pressured teachers for 100 percent Hitler Youth membership, and the teachers, in turn, pressured the students to join. Henry Metelmann's teacher criticized a boy who held out. "You see, all your friends in class have become members," said the teacher. "Surely so many cannot be wrong in their choice while you are the only one who is right. Remember they are all determined to help the Fuhrer."

16   Some teachers quit rather than join the Nazis. Those who refused to quit were dealt with harshly. The Scholl children were upset when the Nazis arrested a young teacher and forced him to stand as Storm Troopers marched past and spat in his face. Afterward, the teacher was taken to a concentration camp.

Excerpted from Hitler Youth: Growing up in Hitler's Shadow *by Susan Campbell Bartoletti, published by Scholastic Inc.*

☁ THINK QUESTIONS   CA-CCSS: CA.RI.8.1, CA.RI.8.4, CA.L.8.4a, CA.L.8.5b, CA.SL.8.1a, CA.SL.8.1b, CA.SL.8.1d

1. Were Sophie's political views in the majority or in the minority among her classmates? Provide textual evidence for your answer.

2. How and why did Sophie's views change as she grew older? Cite evidence for your answer in the text.

3. In addition to the ideas expressed by National Socialism, what motivated students to become active in the Hitler Youth? Support your answer with textual evidence.

4. Use context to determine the meaning of the word **alienated** as it is used in *Hitler Youth: Growing up in Hitler's Shadow.* Write your definition of *alienated* and tell how you found it.

5. Use context, word relationships, and word parts to help you understand the meaning of the word **standardized** in paragraph 9. Write the meaning of *standardized* and explain how you arrived at it.

CLOSE READ
CA-CCSS: CA.RI.8.1, CA.RI.8.2, CA.RI.8.3, CA.RI.8.6, CA.RI.8.8, CA.W.8.4, CA.W.8.5, CA.W.8.6, CA.W.8.10

Reread the excerpt from *Hitler Youth: Growing Up in Hitler's Shadow.* Then use your answers and annotations from the questions to help you complete the Writing Prompt.

 FOCUS QUESTIONS

1. What informational details does the second paragraph reveal that make Sophie seem special? Highlight evidence from the text and make annotations to explain your choices.

2. Describe the conflict between Sophie and the school authorities. What were the reasons behind Sophie's point of view? Support your answer with textual evidence and make annotations to explain your answer choices

3. What role did Adolf Hitler play in the education of Sophie and other German children at the time? Highlight specific textual details and make annotations to support your answer.

4. What is the author's view of the Hitler Youth? How can you tell? In her evaluation of the Hitler Youth, does the author introduce evidence that you feel is irrelevant? Highlight evidence from the text and make annotations to support your explanation.

5. What do Sophie's responses to the Nazis reveal about her? How did she handle the conflict she felt over National Socialism? Highlight textual evidence and make annotations to explain your ideas.

WRITING PROMPT

What is the central or main idea in this excerpt from *Hitler Youth: Growing Up in Hitler's Shadow?* What details does the author use to support this central idea? Use your understanding of informational text elements as well as reasons and evidence to determine the central idea that emerges in this passage. Support your writing with evidence from the text.

Please note that excerpts and passages in the StudySync® library and this workbook are intended as touchstones to generate interest in an author's work. The excerpts and passages do not substitute for the reading of entire texts, and StudySync® strongly recommends that students seek out and purchase the whole literary or informational work in order to experience it as the author intended. Links to online resellers are available in our digital library. In addition, complete works may be ordered through an authorized reseller by filling out and returning to StudySync® the order form enclosed in this workbook.

Reading & Writing Companion   **39**

PARALLEL JOURNEYS

FICTION
Eleanor Ayer
1995

INTRODUCTION

Parallel Journeys weaves together the stories of two young Germans—Alfons Heck, an enthusiastic participant in the Hitler Youth, and Helen Waterford, a Jewish girl who flees to Holland to avoid persecution by the Nazis, only to be captured and sent to Auschwitz death camp. Partially narrated in the protagonists' own words, the book serves as a warning against hatred and discrimination and offers an uplifting message about peace and understanding. The excerpt here focuses on recollections of *Kristallnacht*, the Night of Broken Glass.

"Jewish homes and businesses were destroyed and synagogues burned."

 FIRST READ

From Chapter 4: Kristallnacht: The Night of Broken Glass

1   On the afternoon of November 9, 1938, we were on our way home from school when we ran into small troops of SA and SS men, the Brownshirts and the Blackshirts. We watched open-mouthed as the men jumped off trucks in the marketplace, fanned out in several directions, and began to smash the windows of every Jewish business in Wittlich.

2   Paul Wolff, a local carpenter who belonged to the SS, led the biggest troop, and he pointed out the locations. One of their major targets was Anton Blum's shoe store next to the city hall. Shouting SA men threw hundreds of pairs of shoes into the street. In minutes they were snatched up and carried home by some of the town's nicest families—folks you never dreamed would steal anything.

3   It was *Kristallnacht,* the night of broken glass. For Jews all across Europe, the dark words of warning hurled about by the Nazis suddenly became very real. Just two weeks earlier, thousands of Polish Jews living in Germany had been arrested and shipped back to Poland in boxcars. Among them was the father of seventeen-year-old Herschel Grynszpan, a German Jew who was living in France. Outraged by the Nazis' treatment of his family, Herschel walked into the German Embassy in Paris and shot Ernst vom Rath, the secretary.

4   The murder spawned a night of terror. It was the worst **pogrom**—the most savage attack against the Jews of Germany—thus far in the twentieth century. Leading the attack was the brutal, boorish SS—the *Schutzstaffel.* On their uniforms, SS members wore emblems shaped like double lightening bolts, perfect symbols of the terror and suddenness with which they swooped from the night to arrest their frightened victims.

NOTES

5   Heading the *Schutzstaffel* was Heinrich Himmler who worshipped Adolf Hitler. Himmler was a man of great organizational skills, with a passion for perfect record keeping and a heart as black as his *Schutzstaffel* uniform. His power in the Reich was tremendous; only Hitler **reigned** above him.

6   Working under Himmler to carry out the savagery of *Kristallnacht* was Reinhard Heydrich, the number-two man in the SS. His victims dubbed him "The Blond Beast." Even Hitler called him the man with the iron heart. On direct orders from Heydrich, Jewish homes and businesses were destroyed and **synagogues** burned. "Demonstrations," the SS called the violence, and they informed police that they were to do nothing to stop them.

7   "As many Jews, especially rich ones, are to be arrested as can be accommodated in the prisons," the orders read. Immediately officials at the concentration camps—the special prisons set up by the Nazis—were notified that Jews would be shipped there right away. SS men stormed the streets and searched the attics of Jewish homes, throwing their victim onto trucks to be hauled off to the camps.

8   Four or five of us boys followed Wolff's men when they headed up the *Himmeroder Strasse* toward the Wittlich synagogue. Seconds later the beautiful lead crystal window above the door crashed into the street, and pieces of furniture came flying through doors and windows. A shouting SA man climbed to the roof and waved the rolls of the Torah, the sacred Jewish religious scrolls. "Use it for toilet paper, Jews," he screamed. At that, some people turned shamefacedly away. Most of us stayed, as if **riveted** to the ground, some grinning evilly.

9   It was horribly brutal, but at the same time very exciting to us kids. "Let's go in and smash some stuff," urged my buddy Helmut. With shining eyes, he bent down, picked up a rock and fired it toward one of the windows. I don't know if I would have done the same thing seconds later, but at that moment my Uncle Franz grabbed both of us by the neck, turned us around and kicked us in the seat of the pants. "Get home, you two *Schweinhunde*," he yelled. "What do you think this is, some sort of circus?"

10   Indeed, it was like a beastly, **bizarre** circus of evil. All across Germany the scene was the same. Terror rained down upon the Jews as Nazis took to the streets with axes, hammers, grenades, and guns. According to reports from high Nazi officials, some 20,000 Jews were arrested, 36 killed, and another 36 seriously injured. Thousands of Jews were hauled to concentration camps during *Kristallnacht*. There many died or were beaten severely by Nazi guards who used this chance to take revenge on a hated people.

· · ·

11 Across Europe, Jews panicked as news of the horrors of *Kristallnacht* reached them. In Amsterdam, Helen and Siegfried got their first reports in a phone call from Helen's family.

12   My hometown of Frankfurt, with its 35,000 Jews, had four synagogues. The pogrom started with the burning of the synagogues and all their sacred contents. Jewish stores were destroyed and the windows shattered.

13   Nearly every house was searched for Jewish men. The SA, in plain clothes, came to my parents' apartment to arrest my father and eighteen-year-old brother. A "helpful" neighbor had shown them where in the roomy attic Jews might be hiding. My brother was deported to Buchenwald—a concentration camp near Weimar in eastern Germany—as was Siegfried's brother, Hans.

14 It was not enough for the Jews to suffer destruction of their homes and businesses, beatings and arrests by the SS, and deportation to concentration camps. The Nazis now ordered that the victims must pay for the loss of their own property. The bill for broken glass alone was five million marks. Any insurance money that the Jews might have claimed was taken by the government. And because many of the buildings where Jews had their shops were actually owned by Aryans, the Jews as a group had to pay an additional fine "for their abominable crimes, etc." So declared Hermann Goring, a high-ranking Nazi who was in charge of the German economy. He set their fine at one *billion* marks.

15 For the Jews still left in Germany, the future looked very grim. Many had fled, like Helen and Siegfried, after the first ominous rumblings from Hitler's government. But thousands still remained. These people simply refused to believe that conditions would get any worse. They thought the plight of the Jews would improve, if only they were patient. Helen's father was among them.

16   Although he had lost his business, he was still stubbornly optimistic about the future of the Jews in Germany. Earlier in the summer of 1938 he had been arrested, for no particular reason, and sent to Buchenwald. At that time it was still possible to get people out of a camp if they had a visa to another country. Siegfried and I got permission from the Dutch government for him to come to Holland, but he did not want to leave Germany without his wife and son. Since they had no visas, he stayed with them and waited—until it was almost too late.

Excerpted from *Parallel Journeys* by Eleanor Ayer, published by Aladdin Paperbacks.

Please note that excerpts and passages in the StudySync® library and this workbook are intended as touchstones to generate interest in an author's work. The excerpts and passages do not substitute for the reading of entire texts, and StudySync® strongly recommends that students seek out and purchase the whole literary or informational work in order to experience it as the author intended. Links to online resellers are available in our digital library. In addition, complete works may be ordered through an authorized reseller by filling out and returning to StudySync® the order form enclosed in this workbook.

Reading & Writing Companion   **43**

THINK QUESTIONS   CA-CCSS: CA.RI.8.1, CA.RI.8.4, CA.L.8.4a, CA.L.8.4b

1. What images does the word *Kristallnacht,* or its English translation, "night of broken glass," bring to mind? What words and phrases do the three narrators of the selection—Alfons, Helen, and the author—use that help you form mental pictures of the events happening across Germany on the night of November 9, 1938? Use specific details from the excerpt to support your response.

2. Use details from the text to explain what happened in Germany on *Kristallnacht.*

3. Why did *Kristallnacht* happen? Support your answer, including any inferences you make, with textual evidence.

4. Use context clues in the passage to determine the meaning of the word **bizarre.** Write your definition of *bizarre* and explain how you arrived at it.

5. Remembering that the Greek prefix *syn-* means "together" and the Greek root *agein* means "to lead," use the roots and context clues provided in the excerpt to determine the meaning of **synagogues.** Write your definition of *synagogues* and explain how you arrived at it.

CLOSE READ CA-CCSS: CA.RI.8.1, CA.RI.8.3, CA.RI.8.4, CA.RI.8.6, CA.W.8.3b, CA.W.8.4, CA.W.8.5, CA.W.8.6, CA.W.8.10

Reread the excerpt from *Parallel Journeys.* As you reread, complete the Focus Questions below. Then use your answers and annotations from the questions to help you complete the Writing Prompt.

 FOCUS QUESTIONS

1. How does the author of *Parallel Journeys* make distinctions between Alfons's experience of *Kristallnacht* and Helen's experience? Highlight key details and descriptive language from the text to support your ideas. Make annotations to explain your choices.

2. In Paragraph 16, Ayer discusses the idea that many Jews "simply refused to believe that things would get any worse." Helen echoes this opinion in the next paragraph, commenting that her father "was still stubbornly optimistic about the future." What do you think caused this disconnect between the brutal experience of the pogrom and the persistent optimism Ayer mentions? Support your inferences with textual evidence and make annotations to explain your choices.

3. Think about the three perspectives shown in *Parallel Journeys.* How do Alfons, Helen, and the author communicate information on the same subject? What is the value of the different ways the text makes connections among the ideas, events, and individuals involved? Highlight evidence from the text to support your answer and annotate to explain your choices.

4. Eleanor Ayer, the author of *Parallel Journeys,* chose to intertwine the stories of two people's lives, instead of focusing on only one. What does this choice tell you about her purpose? Highlight evidence from the text to support your explanation.

5. In addition to presenting the narratives of Helen and Alfons, this excerpt from *Parallel Journeys* contains several examples of other people responding to conflict: Herschel Grynszpan, the SA and SS; Helen's father; the "helpful" neighbor in paragraph 14; and so on. Choose one or two groups or individuals and discuss what you learn from them about the conflict. Support your answer with evidence from the text, and annotate the text to show the evidence.

WRITING PROMPT

What can you infer about Alfons and Helen, as adults, from their responses to the events described in *Parallel Journeys* by Eleanor Ayer? Use the informational text elements in this biographical account, including facts, opinions, historical details, and descriptive language to support your inferences. How can contributing to and reading historical accounts like this be useful for people today? Support your response with evidence from the text.

DEAR MISS BREED

NON-FICTION
Joanne Oppenheim
2006

INTRODUCTION

S oon after the Japanese air attack on Pearl Harbor on December 7, 1941, the United States government rounded up more than 110,000 people of Japanese ancestry, most of them American citizens, and placed them in hastily built internment camps. Despite the harsh conditions, dozens of young Japanese Americans found inspiration in the form of a faithful correspondent, advocate, and book supplier: Miss Clara Breed, the Children's Librarian at the San Diego Public Library. In this excerpt from *Dear Miss Breed*, which compiles many of the letters the librarian received from young people she helped, several children have just arrived at the Poston Relocation Center in the blistering hot Arizona desert.

"P.S. There is no water on Sundays."

FIRST READ

NOTES

Excerpt from Chapter Six: Greetings From Far-Off Poston

1   Upon my arrival to the Poston Relocation Center, I stood bewildered, glaring at the hot dusty desert, wondering how we could survive. When my family and I were given our barrack number we spread our blankets and tried to put things in order. The first day here was so hot I should not know how I should express how I felt then. Whoever I met carried wet towels on his heads. Even in the mess hall people ate with wet towels on their heads. Small children had not eaten because of the heat. Even grownups lost their appetite.

2   That night, as I tumbled into bed, I kept thinking how we could ever survive in such a place and how the dusty soil could be made into fertile fields.

3   —Chiyoko Morita, ninth grade

4   After twenty hours on a train and another hour on a hot, dusty bus, the Nikkei arrived at the Poston Relocation Center. It seemed as if they had reached the ends of the earth. To get an idea of how removed from their former lives they must have felt: The nearest town, Parker, Arizona, was sixteen miles away and it had just one telephone! If one were driving toward California, the first service station would be eighty miles away.

5   It was so hot on the bus that they had opened the windows, only to be covered by powdery white dust the consistency of flour. When they stepped off the buses, friends didn't recognize one another. When they arrived in the **torrid** heat of summer, at **barracks** that were not complete, their hopes that Poston would be an improvement over Santa Anita were dashed. It was ten degrees hotter than the Libyan desert.

6   The buildings had no window screens but plenty of bugs, there was a record-breaking temperature of more than 120 degrees, and windstorms coated everything with fine sand. Almost overnight, Poston became the third-largest community in Arizona. Where there had been nothing, a city of tar-papered barracks was hastily built to house more than eighteen thousand Nikkei. The camp was named for Charles D. Poston, the first congressman from the Territory of Arizona and first superintendent of Indian affairs in Arizona. In 1865, he had helped to establish the Colorado River Reservation.

7   Built on Indian land, Poston was the largest of all ten relocation centers. It was divided into three parts, officially known as Poston I, II, and III. Five thousand workers on a double work shift constructed the camps in record time. In fact, one builder boasted that they had erected sixteen barracks in twenty-two minutes! Due to a shortage of wood, barracks were built with green pine that shrank and left cracks between the boards, allowing sand and insects to seep and creep inside. The heat was so extreme that standard army barracks were redesigned with double roofs for insulation. But even double roofs did not block the oppressive heat. No guard towers were built at Poston since the location was "in the middle of nowhere" and towers were considered unnecessary.

8   As buses pulled in, a monitor climbed on board to explain how they were to line up for housing and registration. They arrived at odd hours, some in the middle of the night. People had endured a long, hot trip with poor food. They were weak from heat and dust. The shock of the whole experience was **overwhelming.** Still, a line had to be formed at the mess hall as the head of each family registered. Everyone over seventeen was fingerprinted and had to sign an agreement that he or she would live by the regulations of the center and work. Another line was formed in the recreation hall for housing assignments.

9   Even nine-year-old Jack Watanabe felt cut off from the world: "We are now in a strange place—Poston, Arizona. I doubt whether this is even on the map."

10 Afraid that there would not be enough housing to go around, the administration put four to eight people into a single room, twenty by twenty-five feet. In Poston III there were eighteen blocks. Each block had fourteen barracks with separate **latrines** and showers for men and women, a mess hall, a laundry and ironing room, and a recreation hall. Since there had to be a minimum of four people in an apartment, small families had to share a single room with another family. Almost all the San Diegans were sent to Poston III. Fusa and her mother had to live with another San Diego family until there were more barracks.

Copyright © BookheadEd Learning, LLC

NOTES

11 Don Elberson, a sociologist who worked for the War Relocation Authority at Poston, could never erase his memory of the misery families encountered when they arrived:

12 It was brutal. Some days we had to process five hundred or more people. . . . But nothing **mitigated** the moment when I had to take them to their new homes. . . . You'd have to take these people into this dingy excuse for a room, twenty by twenty-five feet at best. These were people who'd left everything behind, sometimes fine houses. I learned after the first day not to enter with the family, but to stand outside. It was too terrible to witness the pain in people's faces, too shameful for them to be seen in this degrading situation.

13 Fourteen-year-old Babe Karasawa never forgot that moment. Here's how he described it to me sixty years later:

14 We opened the doors of our barrack and there were weeds growing between the spaces in the floorboards . . . they were three feet tall inside the barrack! I remember that because my two brothers and I, we just ripped those weeds out. We took buckets of water and washed all over the walls—we washed the dust and the grit. All the water goes right between the spaces—through the floorboards—the place is dry in thirty minutes because it was just so hot. This was the end of August in '42. The records show that in '42, in the middle of July, they had a record temperature of 144 degrees! I used to walk like this . . . my head tilted down and sideways so my face wouldn't go straight into the heat. When I drank water, it would just come right out of my arms. . . . Perspiration just poured right out. This was during the hottest time and I used to always have heat rash.

15 In her first letter from Poston, Louise tries hard to hold on to her rosy view of the world, but finding positive things to say about Poston was challenging. Now she not only missed San Diego; she missed Santa Anita! Still, sixteen-year-old Louise manages to see beauty in the bleakness.

16 *August 27, 1942*

17 *Dear Miss Breed,*

18 *Greetings from far-off Poston, Arizona! We arrived yesterday about 3:30 P.M. It was a very long train ride. . . . After leaving Barstow, we began to feel the heat. They say yesterday was a cool day but to us it was extremely hot.*

19 *We traveled through desert after desert. There were many houses which looked as if they were built many years ago. We seldom saw a*

human being except when passing through a small town. One of the most beautiful scenery was when crossing a bridge which was right above the Colorado River. It is, indeed, a beautiful river.

20   *One common thing you see while coming here is—the beds and beddings are all placed outside the homes. It has been said that the heat is so hot that the people all sleep outside. It is very hot here. We traveled by bus through acres of cotton plants—so you can imagine the heat because cotton has to be grown in a hot climate.*

21   *After leaving the train, we had to travel by bus—about 20 miles. We are in Camp No. 3. It is not quite yet completed. It is so sandy here that everyone's hair looks gray. Sometimes the wind blows but when it does the sand comes with it. This camp is so far away from civilization that it makes me feel as if I was a convict who is not allowed to see anyone. I'd much rather sleep in the Santa Anita horse stables—this has made me realize how fortunate I was to be able to live in Santa Anita. The nearest town which is a very tiny one is about 20 miles away. This trip has made me realize the wonderful work of nature. Her delicate work in shaping the stone mountains, the beautiful coloring of the surroundings— it seemed as if I was looking at the picture or a painting of a genius.*

22   *This place differs greatly from . . . Santa Anita. In Santa Anita we were allowed to keep a bucket and a broom in our homes until the time came to leave but in Poston we are allowed to BORROW a bucket, broom or mop for 1/2 hrs. This makes it very inconvenient because often they run out of them and we have to wait until one is returned. Even in the dining rooms we have to take our own spoons and forks. They provide just the knife and cups + plates and, of course, food. Yesterday I ate rice, weenies, and cabbage with a knife. That was a new experience for me! You never realize how valuable a thing is until you experience it. The dining rooms are very small here because there is one to each block.*

23   *. . . We have to mop the house every day because of the dust but it does not do any good because before you know it it's dusty again.*

24   *My, this letter is getting too long and it's probably getting boring so I'll write again soon. If you have any questions, I'll be glad to answer them if I am able.*

25   *Most sincerely,*

26   *Louise Ogawa*

27   *P.S. There is no water on Sundays. The electricity is also turned off. Sunday morning everyone eats before 6:00 A.M. Water and electricity*

turned off between 6:00 A.M. to 6:00 P.M. on Sundays. Very very inconvenient. Never realized how valuable water is. The place looked deserted all the time because of the sandiness every[one] stays inside and no one is outside—not even the children so it looks as if no one lives in the barracks.

28 In spite of all the difficulties, Louise's positive and patriotic spirit rings true in these final words of her letter: "If American soldiers can endure hardships so can we!"

From DEAR MISS BREED by Joanne Oppenheim. Scholastic Inc./Nonfiction. Copyright © 2006 by Joanne Oppenheim. Reprinted by permission.

 THINK QUESTIONS   CA-CCSS: CA.RI.8.1, CA.RI.8.4, CA.L.8.4a, CA.L.8.4b

1. Why were more than 110,000 people of Japanese ancestry in the United States relocated to places such as the Poston Relocation Center in Arizona? Include evidence from the Introduction and the text of this excerpt to explain your inferences.

2. Describe the conditions at the Poston Relocation Center. What made living there so difficult? Use specific details from *Dear Miss Breed* in your answer.

3. Don Elberson was a sociologist who worked for the War Relocation Authority. What was his job at the Poston Relocation Center, and why did he find it so difficult? Support your answer with textual evidence.

4. Use context to determine the meaning of the word **barracks** as it is used in *Dear Miss Breed*. Write your definition of *barracks* and explain how you arrived at it.

5. Remembering that the Latin root *mitis* means "to soften," use this knowledge as well as context clues in the passage to determine the meaning of **mitigated.** Write your definition of *mitigated* and explain how you arrived at it.

CLOSE READ   CA-CCSS: CA.RI.8.1, CA.RI.8.3, CA.RI.8.7, CA.RI.8.9, CA.W.8.1

Reread the excerpt from *Dear Miss Breed*. As you reread, complete the Focus Questions below. Then use your answers and annotations from the questions to help you complete the Writing Prompt.

FOCUS QUESTIONS

1. *Dear Miss Breed* contains eyewitness accounts in two different media: Babe and Chiyoko's oral history interviews, in which they recall events from many years later, and Louise's letter to Miss Breed. Babe and Chiyoko both make very strong statements about the worst aspects of Poston: the unrelenting heat, the dust, and the poor quality of the housing provided. Contrast these two oral history interviews with Louise's letter. How does the letter differ from the interview statements in content and tone, and what conclusions can you draw by contrasting these two different media? Annotate the text and use specific details from the passages in your response.

2. Like Milton Eisenhower, Don Elberson worked for the War Relocation Authority. Compare and contrast Elberson's statement in *Dear Miss Breed* with Eisenhower's narration in the newsreel. How does each account enrich your understanding of the other? How do you explain the differences in the content of the two accounts? Use specific details from the passage and the newsreel to support your response.

3. The various interview statements, Louise's letter, and author Joanne Oppenheim's commentary contain many visual details that describe the Poston relocation center. The War Relocation Office newsreel gives you the opportunity to see film footage of the actual camp. How does the video compare to the mental images you formed while reading *Dear Miss Breed*? Use specific details from the text and newsreel in your response.

4. The Poston Relocation Center was named for Charles D. Poston, the first congressman from the Territory of Arizona and first superintendent of Indian affairs in Arizona. Why do you think the the government chose to name the relocation center after this man? What parallels can you find between the government's treatment of Japanese and Native Americans? Cite evidence from the text in your response.

5. With the attack on Pearl Harbor, a serious conflict arose between the U.S. government and the Japanese Americans living in California. Government officials felt they had to weigh the country's wartime security against the civil and constitutional rights of Japanese Americans in California. Louise's letter to Miss Breed shows her response to this conflict. What does Louise's response say about the kind of person she is? Use specific details from the text to support your response.

WRITING PROMPT

Louise Ogawa, Babe Karasawa, Don Elberson, Chiyoko Morita, and Jack Watanabe all provide firsthand accounts of the relocation camp in Poston. What makes firsthand accounts of historical events more interesting and exciting than descriptions by people who weren't present at the scene? How do firsthand accounts help you visualize places and events in the past in a way that secondhand accounts do not? Support your writing with evidence from the text.

Please note that excerpts and passages in the StudySync® library and this workbook are intended as touchstones to generate interest in an author's work. The excerpts and passages do not substitute for the reading of entire texts, and StudySync® strongly recommends that students seek out and purchase the whole literary or informational work in order to experience it as the author intended. Links to online resellers are available in our digital library. In addition, complete works may be ordered through an authorized reseller by filling out and returning to StudySync® the order form enclosed in this workbook.

Reading & Writing
Companion

53

NOBEL PRIZE ACCEPTANCE SPEECH

NON-FICTION
Elie Wiesel
1986

INTRODUCTION

Elie Wiesel was a survivor of the Auschwitz and Buchenwald Nazi concentration camps, going on to write 57 books on the Holocaust and other subjects. The Nobel Committee called him a "messenger to mankind," stating that his struggle to come to terms with "his own personal experience of total humiliation and of the utter contempt for humanity shown in Hitler's death camps," as well as his "practical work in the cause of peace," delivered a powerful message "of peace, atonement, and human dignity" to humanity. The following is an excerpt from his acceptance speech.

"...if we forget, we are guilty, we are accomplices."

 ## FIRST READ

 NOTES

1   And it is with a profound sense of **humility** that I accept the honor—the highest there is—that you have chosen to bestow upon me. I know your choice transcends my person.

2   Do I have the right to represent the **multitudes** who have perished? Do I have the right to accept this great honor on their behalf? I do not. No one may speak for the dead, no one may interpret their mutilated dreams and visions. And yet, I sense their presence. I always do—and at this moment more than ever. The presence of my parents, that of my little sister. The presence of my teachers, my friends, my companions....

3   This honor belongs to all the survivors and their children and, through us to the Jewish people with whose destiny I have always identified.

4   I remember: it happened yesterday, or eternities ago. A young Jewish boy discovered the Kingdom of Night. I remember his bewilderment, I remember his anguish. It all happened so fast. The ghetto. The **deportation.** The sealed cattle car. The fiery altar upon which the history of our people and the future of mankind were meant to be sacrificed.

5   I remember he asked his father: "Can this be true? This is the twentieth century, not the Middle Ages. Who would allow such crimes to be committed? How could the world remain silent?"

6   And now the boy is turning to me. "Tell me," he asks, "what have you done with my future, what have you done with your life?"

7   And I tell him that I have tried. That I have tried to keep memory alive, that I have tried to fight those who would forget. Because if we forget, we are guilty, we are accomplices.

Please note that excerpts and passages in the StudySync® library and this workbook are intended as touchstones to generate interest in an author's work. The excerpts and passages do not substitute for the reading of entire texts, and StudySync® strongly recommends that students seek out and purchase the whole literary or informational work in order to experience it as the author intended. Links to online resellers are available in our digital library. In addition, complete works may be ordered through an authorized reseller by filling out and returning to StudySync® the order form enclosed in this workbook.

Reading & Writing
Companion

55

8   And then I explain to him how **naïve** we were, that the world did know and remained silent. And that is why I swore never to be silent whenever wherever human beings endure suffering and humiliation. We must take sides. Neutrality helps the oppressor, never the victim. Silence encourages the tormentor, never the tormented. Sometimes we must interfere. When human lives are endangered, when human dignity is in jeopardy, national borders and sensitivities become irrelevant. Wherever men and women are persecuted because of their race, religion, or political views, that place must—at that moment—become the center of the universe.

9   Human rights are being **violated** on every continent. More people are oppressed than free. How can one not be sensitive to their plight? Human suffering anywhere concerns men and women everywhere...

10   There is so much to be done, there is so much that can be done. One person—a Raoul Wallenberg, an Albert Schweitzer, Martin Luther King, Jr.— one person of integrity, can make a difference, a difference of life and death.

11   As long as one dissident is in prison, our freedom will not be true. As long as one child is hungry, our life will be filled with anguish and shame. What all these victims need above all is to know that they are not alone; that we are not forgetting them, that when their voices are stifled we shall lend them ours, that while their freedom depends on ours, the quality of our freedom depends on theirs.

12   This is what I say to the young Jewish boy wondering what I have done with his years. It is in his name that I speak to you and that I express to you my deepest gratitude as one who has emerged from the Kingdom of Night. We know that every moment is a moment of grace, every hour an offering; not to share them would mean to betray them.

13   Our lives no longer belong to us alone; they belong to all those who need us desperately.

THINK QUESTIONS CA-CCSS: CA.RI.8.1, CA.L.8.4a, CA.L.8.4b, CA.SL.8.1a, CA.SL.8.1c, CA.SL.8.1d

1. Who is the young boy who "discovered the Kingdom of Night" in paragraph 4? Use evidence from the text and your knowledge of Wiesel's history to support your answer.

2. What does Wiesel mean when he says in paragraph 7, "Because if we forget, we are guilty, we are accomplices"? Use evidence from the text to support your answer.

3. Write two or three sentences about what Wiesel is calling on his listeners to do. What responsibility does he give to those who listen? Support your answer with textual evidence.

4. Remembering that *multi* is a Latin root meaning "much or many," use this knowledge and context to determine the meaning of the word **multitudes** as it is used in the passage. Write your definition of *multitudes* and tell how you found it.

5. Use context to determine the meaning of the word **violated** as it is used in the passage. Write your synonyms of *violated* here and tell how you found them.

CLOSE READ

CA-CCSS: CA.RI.8.1, CA.RI.8.2, CA.RI.8.3, CA.RI.8.7, CA.W.8.2b, CA.W.8.4, CA.W.8.5, CA.W.8.10

Reread the excerpt from Elie Wiesel's "Nobel Acceptance Speech." As you reread, complete the Focus Questions below. Then use your answers and annotations from the questions to help you complete the Writing Prompt.

FOCUS QUESTIONS

1. How does the medium of video compare to reading a text version of Wiesel's "Nobel Acceptance Speech"? Focus on the first three paragraphs. Highlight examples from the text and annotate to <u>make comparisons to the video</u>, 3:04-4:59.

2. What does Wiesel mean by "the Kingdom of Night"? How does this image help reveal Wiesel's point of view in paragraphs 4–7? Highlight evidence from the text and annotate to explain the connections to his point of view.

3. What is the central idea of paragraph 8? What does Wiesel mean when he begins the paragraph, "And then I explain to him how naïve we were..."? Highlight examples from the text that illustrate this central idea. Then annotate to explain your answer.

4. What is Wiesel's purpose for delivering his speech? Highlight evidence from the last five paragraphs (9–13) of the text that will support your understanding. Annotate to explain how these details reveal the author's purpose.

5. According to Wiesel, what did the worldwide response to the Holocaust teach him about the world when he was still a young man? What does he feel the world's reaction should be when it faces future conflicts? Highlight evidence from the text and annotate to explain your ideas.

WRITING PROMPT

How does the experience of reading the text of Elie Wiesel's "Nobel Prize Acceptance Speech" differ from the experience of watching the video of the speech? How do the visual and audio components of the video affect the message of the speech? Support your writing with evidence from both the video and the speech.

REMARKS
IN MEMORY OF
THE VICTIMS OF THE HOLOCAUST

NON-FICTION
Ban Ki-Moon
2013

INTRODUCTION

Ban Ki-moon is the eighth Secretary-General of the United Nations. He explained his call to serve the world's poorest and most vulnerable people as being rooted in his own experience: "I grew up in war and saw the United Nations help my country to recover and rebuild. That experience was a big part of what led me to pursue a career in public service." In the speech here, which was delivered at Park East Synagogue in New York City at a memorial for Holocaust victims, Ban famously asks, "Each time we hear 'never again', but can we truly say we have learned the lessons of these tragedies?"

"The language of hatred is corrosive and contagious."

 FIRST READ

Rabbi Schneier,
President Hochberg,
Excellencies,
Ladies and gentlemen,

1   Shabat **Shalom.** Salaam. Peace to you all.

2   It is a great honour to be with you once again.

3   Thank you, Rabbi Schneier, for your gracious introduction. I hope every day to live up to your high praise and expectations.

4   On this day when we remember the victims of the Holocaust, let me pay special tribute to the survivors who have joined us.

5   Rabbi Schneier knows fully their pain and suffering, for he too is a survivor.

6   For most of us it is hard to imagine the anguish of knowing that you and your loved ones have been singled out to die because of your faith, your culture or your race.

7   Yet, this is the stark truth.

8   In the Second World War, Jews, Roma and Sinti, homosexuals, communists, the mentally ill—anyone who did not conform to Hitler's perverted ideology of Aryan perfection—were systematically persecuted, rounded up and transported to death camps.

9   Some were murdered immediately; others cruelly worked to death.

10 Such an operation takes extensive organization. It takes many people—from leaders to ordinary citizens—to participate, cooperate or simply turn a blind eye.

11   This is perhaps the greatest tragedy of **genocide**—and the reason why we must be ever vigilant.

12   The language of hatred is corrosive and contagious. Its moral corruption can eat into hearts and minds in even the most progressive or sophisticated societies.

13   The more often you hear that your neighbour is vile, subhuman, not worthy of the rights that you take for granted, the greater the chance of such beliefs taking root.

14   That is why I spoke so frankly and forcefully last year in Tehran about Holocaust denial.

15   It is why Rabbi Schneier and I and so many others are so committed to the United Nations Alliance of Civilizations.

16   Neither anti-Semitism nor Islamophobia nor other such forms of bias have a place in the 21st century world we are trying to build.

17   This is also why I worry about the continued stalemate in negotiations between Israel and the Palestinians.

18   We now have a whole generation of young people on both sides who risk growing up with a demonized, dehumanized—and utterly false—concept of their neighbours.

19   They need to be educated to co-exist peacefully with their neighbours.

20   The only way to build peace is to build bridges and break down walls.

21   Doing so will take courage, but it must be done.

22   This year, the United Nations has chosen "the courage to care" as the theme of the International Day of Commemoration in Memory of the Victims of the Holocaust.

23   We are honouring those who risked their lives and their families to save Jews and other victims of persecution from almost certain death.

24   Some, like Raoul Wallenberg, are household names.

25   But most are unsung heroes—brave men and women from all walks of life, and many nations. Teenagers and parents, parliamentarians and priests, journalists and diplomats—all had the courage to care.

Please note that excerpts and passages in the StudySync® library and this workbook are intended as touchstones to generate interest in an author's work. The excerpts and passages do not substitute for the reading of entire texts, and StudySync® strongly recommends that students seek out and purchase the whole literary or informational work in order to experience it as the author intended. Links to online resellers are available in our digital library. In addition, complete works may be ordered through an authorized reseller by filling out and returning to StudySync® the order form enclosed in this workbook.

Reading & Writing
Companion   61

26   Their example is as relevant today as ever—which is why the United Nations has produced an education kit for teachers to tell their story.

27   In a world where extremist acts of violence and hatred capture the headlines on an almost daily basis, we need to take inspiration from these ordinary people who took extraordinary steps to defend human dignity.

28   Ladies and gentlemen,

29   Last year I visited Srebrenica, the site of the worst act of genocide in Europe since the Holocaust.

30   I visited the graves and wept with the mothers of the slain.

31   It is not an easy place for a United Nations Secretary-General to visit.

32   The United Nations—the international community—failed to protect thousands of Bosnian Muslim men and boys from slaughter.

33   The shadow of Srebrenica has joined that of Rwanda, Cambodia, the Holocaust.

34   Each time we hear "never again."

35   But can we truly say we have learned the lessons of these tragedies?

36   As an international community, do we have the courage to care—and the resolve to act?

37   In 2005 the United Nations General Assembly—at the level of Heads of State and Governments—adopted the responsibility to protect.

38   It is a landmark concept. It puts the obligation firmly on States to protect their populations from genocide, crimes against humanity, war crimes or ethnic cleansing.

39   And in the face of these crimes and violations there is a corresponding duty of the international community to act.

40   The responsibility to protect applies everywhere and all the time. It has been implemented with success in a number of places, including in Libya and Côte d'Ivoire.

41   But today it faces a great test in Syria.

42   More than 60,000 people have now died in a conflict whose seeds lie in the peaceful demand of people for greater freedom.

43 We have seen a government brutally and mercilessly oppress dissent and fan the flames of a civil war that threatens to bring instability to a whole region.

44 I have repeatedly called for unity from the Security Council to decisively address this tragedy.

45 So too has the General Assembly—by an overwhelming majority.

46 Each day brings more suffering.

47 I met some of the refugees last month, in camps in Jordan and Turkey.

48 I talked to families who had fled with just what they could carry; children whose future has been thrown into uncertainty.

49 They told me that all they wanted was to go home and live in safety and security.

50 Today's theme challenges us: do we have the courage to care?

51 I am deeply concerned about the situation in Syria not simply because of the terrible suffering, but because of what may come next.

52 Each day's delay in resolving the crisis raises the spectre of the violence spreading along religious and ethnic lines.

53 Each day's delay sees new **atrocities** by both sides. It is essential that all perpetrators of international crimes understand that they will be held to account.

54 There will be no amnesties for those most responsible.

55 The old era of impunity is ending. In its place, slowly but surely, we are building a new age of accountability.

56 But the important thing is to end the violence in Syria—now—and begin the process of transition.

57 Too much blood has been shed. It is time for **reconciliation.**

58 There is a proverb that says: if you want revenge you should dig two graves.

59 Syria will need many men and women of courage who will reject revenge and embrace peace.

60 People like Rabbi Schneier.

Please note that excerpts and passages in the StudySync® library and this workbook are intended as touchstones to generate interest in an author's work. The excerpts and passages do not substitute for the reading of entire texts, and StudySync® strongly recommends that students seek out and purchase the whole literary or informational work in order to experience it as the author intended. Links to online resellers are available in our digital library. In addition, complete works may be ordered through an authorized reseller by filling out and returning to StudySync® the order form enclosed in this workbook.

Reading & Writing
Companion

63

61 He too visited Srebrenica last year.

62 He spoke in solidarity—as only someone who has shared indescribable suffering can.

63 And this is what he said:

64 "As a survivor I neither turned against man or God. Instead, in memory of my family and the many millions **exterminated** like them, I devoted my life to help build bridges between all of God's children in pursuit of peace and justice." End of quote.

65 Such forgiveness takes courage—the courage to see what is right and to do it.

66 Whatever one's faith, this is our duty—as individuals, as communities and as nations.

67 We have a responsibility to protect.

68 We must have the courage to care.

69 Thank you.

THINK QUESTIONS CA-CCSS: CA.RI.8.1, CA.RI.8.4, CA.L.8.4a, CA.L.8.4b

1. What does Ban Ki-moon mean when he uses the term "Aryan perfection" in his speech? Use evidence from the text to explain your inference.

2. Write two or three sentences explaining why the speaker believes hate speech, or the "language of hatred," causes problems. Support your answer with textual evidence.

3. Refer to one or more details from the text to support your understanding of why Ban Ki-moon wept on his visit to Srebrenica. In your evidence include ideas that are directly stated in the text as well as ideas that you have inferred from clues in the text.

4. Use context to determine the meaning of the word **atrocities** as it is used in "Remarks in Memory of the Victims of The Holocaust." Write your definition of *atrocities* and tell how you found it.

5. Use the context clues provided in the passage to determine the meaning of **shalom.** Write your definition of *shalom* and tell how you got it.

CLOSE READ
CA-CCSS: CA.RI.8.1, CA.RI.8.2, CA.RI.8.3, CA.RI.8.4, CA.RI.8.5, CA.RI.8.6, CA.RI.8.8, CA.W.8.2

Reread the text "Remarks in Memory of the Victims of The Holocaust." As you reread, complete the Focus Questions below. Then use your answers and annotations from the questions to help you complete the Writing Prompt.

FOCUS QUESTIONS

1. In about the middle of his speech, in the 34th paragraph, Ban Ki-moon recites two sentences: "Each time we hear 'never again.' But can we truly say we have learned the lessons of these tragedies?" Why does he place such a focus on what people say and how does he use these questions to reinforce the text structure of problem and solution?

2. Ban Ki-moon states that the Holocaust was an operation that demanded extensive organization and the participation of many people was needed to carry it out. In addition, too many people did nothing to try and stop it. What evidence does Ki-moon offer that this is still true today?

3. In discussing his visit to Srebrenica, Ban Ki-moon says he "wept with the mothers of the slain" and admits that Srebrenica is "not an easy place for a United Nations Secretary-General to visit." What is the effect of those statements on the tone of the speech? Highlight your textual evidence and make annotations to explain your choices.

4. At various points in the speech, Ban Ki-moon interjects himself into the events he is describing and the point he is making. How does he do this and what is his purpose in stressing his point of view?

5. What does Ban Ki-moon suggest the world do about genocide whenever it threatens to occur? What specific responses to dangerous conflicts does he suggest?

WRITING PROMPT

What details does Ban Ki-moon include to support his purpose and point of view? Which details help create the tone of the speech? Use your understanding of informational text structure to determine how details in this speech support Ban Ki-moon's point of view. Include text evidence from the speech to support your response.

Please note that excerpts and passages in the StudySync® library and this workbook are intended as touchstones to generate interest in an author's work. The excerpts and passages do not substitute for the reading of entire texts, and StudySync® strongly recommends that students seek out and purchase the whole literary or informational work in order to experience it as the author intended. Links to online resellers are available in our digital library. In addition, complete works may be ordered through an authorized reseller by filling out and returning to StudySync® the order form enclosed in this workbook.

Reading & Writing Companion

65

A LETTER FROM ROBERT

English Language
Development

DRAMA

INTRODUCTION

This short play takes place in London after the Blitz, a period of intense bombing by the German Air Force during World War II. The Blitz, which lasted eight months from September 1940 to May 1941, destroyed or damaged over one million homes and killed more than 40,000 civilians. In the drama, a grieving mother returns to London after the bombing has ended, only to find that her home has been destroyed.

"...I'll always wish to see him coming around the corner, but I never will."

 FIRST READ

1 [*A **residential** street in London. It is early morning on a day in July 1941. We see two tall buildings, damaged but standing. Rubble from a third building lies between them. MARGARET takes cautious steps toward the **debris**. When she reaches the spot that used to be her doorstep, she weeps. The front door of one of the buildings swings open, and HELEN steps out.*]

2 HELEN: I was starting to think I'd never see you again!

3 MARGARET *(jumping and wiping away tears)*: You **startled** me. I'm relieved to see you've survived. Attacking military bases during a war is one thing. But bombing innocent civilians? I had to go. I promised Robert I'd stay safe . . . You should have come to my sister's to wait out the attacks.

4 HELEN: It will take more than incendiary bombs to scare me. I was lucky. Broken windows and a hole in the wall. Nothing that can't be fixed. You have my sympathy about your house. You can stay with me until this **dreadful** war ends. No sense in starting construction now.

5 MARGARET *(sadly)*: I am not rebuilding. I am leaving London.

6 HELEN *(with surprise)*: You can't leave! Who will your son come home to after the war if you're not here?

7 MARGARET: My son won't be coming home. I received a telegram from the Royal Air Force. Robert was killed in combat.

8 HELEN: Stay with me. We will get through this together.

9 MARGARET: There are too many memories. Everywhere there's something that reminds me . . . I'll always wish to see him coming around the corner, but I never will. There is nothing left for me here.

10   HELEN: Some of your things survived the blast. [HELEN *pulls a letter out of her pocket.*]

11   MARGARET: It's Robert's letter. [*begins to read*] The twenty-second of May, nineteen forty. My dearest mother, two days ago our Prime Minister gave a radio address urging us to ready ourselves for **defense** during these terrible times. These past two days I have thought of little else.

12   [*As MARGARET reads, another voice joins hers, as if coming from a ghost. It is ROBERT'S VOICE.*]

13   MARGARET and ROBERT: I have thought about the German attacks in France, Denmark, Norway, Belgium, and the Netherlands. As much as it pains me to leave you, Mother, I know their pain is greater.

14   [*MARGARET'S VOICE dies out, and ROBERT'S VOICE continues alone.*]

15   ROBERT'S VOICE: It is my duty as a citizen of the world to rise up and fight against the forces of evil that are spreading across the continent. I will take my place among the brave men of the Royal Air Force. I will fight for Britain, for Europe, and, most of all, for you.

USING LANGUAGE CA-CCSS: ELD.PII.8.1.Ex

Complete the chart by sorting the items from the options below into those that are characters, those that are stage directions, and those that are dialogue.

Options		
Stay with me. We will get through this together.	[MARGARET *takes cautious steps toward the debris.*]	[MARGARET'S VOICE *dies out, and* ROBERT'S VOICE *continues alone.*]
I am leaving London.	ROBERT	Broken windows and a hole in the wall. Nothing that can't be fixed.
MARGARET	[HELEN *pulls a letter out of her pocket.*]	HELEN

Characters	Stage Directions	Dialogue

Please note that excerpts and passages in the StudySync® library and this workbook are intended as touchstones to generate interest in an author's work. The excerpts and passages do not substitute for the reading of entire texts, and StudySync® strongly recommends that students seek out and purchase the whole literary or informational work in order to experience it as the author intended. Links to online resellers are available in our digital library. In addition, complete works may be ordered through an authorized reseller by filling out and returning to StudySync® the order form enclosed in this workbook.

Reading & Writing Companion **69**

MEANINGFUL INTERACTIONS CA-CCSS: ELD.PI.8.1.Ex

Work with your group to discuss your first impressions of the text. First, take turns saying what you think about the characters, the setting, and Margaret's decision to leave London. Then, build on your peers' responses by asking questions and explaining why you agree or disagree with their ideas. Use the speaking frames to support your discussion. Last, use the self-assessment rubric to evaluate your participation in the discussion.

- In my opinion, Margaret / Helen / Robert is . . . because . . .

- In my opinion, London after the Blitz is . . . because . . .

- I think Margaret wants to leave London because . . .

- I think you said . . . Why do you think that?

- I agree / disagree because . . .

 ## SELF-ASSESSMENT RUBRIC CA-CCSS: ELD.PI.8.1.Ex

	4 I did this well.	3 I did this pretty well.	2 I did this a little bit.	1 I did not do this.
I took an active part with others in doing the assigned task.				
I contributed effectively to the group's discussion.				
I waited my turn to speak.				
I asked group members questions about their ideas.				
I built on my group members' responses by explaining why I agreed or disagreed with their ideas.				

REREAD

Reread paragraphs 1–8 of "A Letter from Robert." After you reread, complete the Using Language and Meaningful Interactions activities.

USING LANGUAGE CA-CCSS: ELD.PI.8.6.c.Ex

Read each word, the root, and affix meanings in the first three columns. Complete each row by filling in the correct definition from the Definition Options box.

Definition Options	
regular people; not members of the military	the process of building something
the feeling of support for someone else	relating to a weapon that sets fires
not deserving of harm	

Word	Root Meaning	Affix Meaning	Definition
innocent	*noc-* meaning "harm"	*in-* meaning "not"	
civilians	*civ-* meaning "citizen"	*-an* meaning "one that is"	
incendiary	*cend-* meaning "glowing"	*in-* meaning "on" *-ary* meaning "relating to"	
sympathy	*path-* meaning "feeling"	*sym-* meaning "with"	
construction	*struct-* meaning "build"	*con-* meaning "with" *-ion* meaning "act or process"	

Reading & Writing
Companion

MEANINGFUL INTERACTIONS CA-CCSS: ELD.PI.8.1.Ex

Based on what you have read in "A Letter from Robert," how do you think each character feels about London and the war? What textual evidence supports your ideas? Work in small groups to practice asking relevant questions and answering those questions using textual evidence. Use the speaking frames to support your discussion. Then, use the self-assessment rubric to evaluate your participation in the discussion.

- In my opinion, Margaret / Helen / Robert feels . . . about the war because . . .

- In my opinion, Margaret / Helen feels . . . about London because . . .

- The characters' perspectives are alike / different because . . .

- What text evidence do you base your ideas on? Is it . . . ?

- You said . . . , but did you consider . . . ?

- What else does the text say about . . . ?

SELF-ASSESSMENT RUBRIC CA-CCSS: ELD.PI.8.1.Ex

	4 I did this well.	3 I did this pretty well.	2 I did this a little bit.	1 I did not do this.
I expressed my ideas clearly.				
I used textual evidence to support my ideas.				
I asked relevant questions during the discussion.				
I answered questions using textual evidence.				

REREAD

Reread paragraphs 9–15 of "A Letter from Robert." After you reread, complete the Using Language and Meaningful Interactions activities.

USING LANGUAGE CA-CCSS: ELD.PII.8.5.Ex

Fill in the blanks to complete the sentences about the characters in the play.

1. **Find the sentence in paragraph 9 that tells what Margaret wishes.**

   I'll _____ wish to see him coming _____.

2. **Find the sentence in paragraph 10 that tells where Helen gets the letter.**

   HELEN pulls a letter _____.

3. **Find the sentence in paragraph 11 that tells how people ready themselves for war.**

   ... our Prime Minister gave a radio address urging us to ready ourselves _____

   _____.

4. **Find the sentence in paragraph 15 that shows what Robert thinks his duty is.**

   It is my duty _____ to rise up and fight _____

   _____ that are spreading _____.

5. **Find the sentence in paragraph 15 that shows what Robert will fight for.**

   I will fight _____, _____, and, most of all, _____.

MEANINGFUL INTERACTIONS CA-CCSS: ELD.PI.8.11.a.Ex

In "A Letter from Robert," Robert decides to join the Royal Air Force, Helen decides to stay in London during the Blitz, and Margaret decides to leave London after she loses her son and her home. Choose one character and tell whether or not you agree with his or her decision. What evidence from the text supports your opinion? Work in small groups to practice sharing and discussing your opinions, using the speaking frames.

- I agree / disagree with Robert's / Helen's / Margaret's decision to . . . because . . .

- My opinion is based on . . .

Please note that excerpts and passages in the StudySync® library and this workbook are intended as touchstones to generate interest in an author's work. The excerpts and passages do not substitute for the reading of entire works, and StudySync® strongly recommends that students seek out and purchase the whole literary or informational work in order to experience it as the author intended. Links to online resellers are available in our digital library. In addition, complete works may be ordered through an authorized reseller by filling out and returning to StudySync® the order form enclosed in this workbook.

Reading & Writing
Companion

73

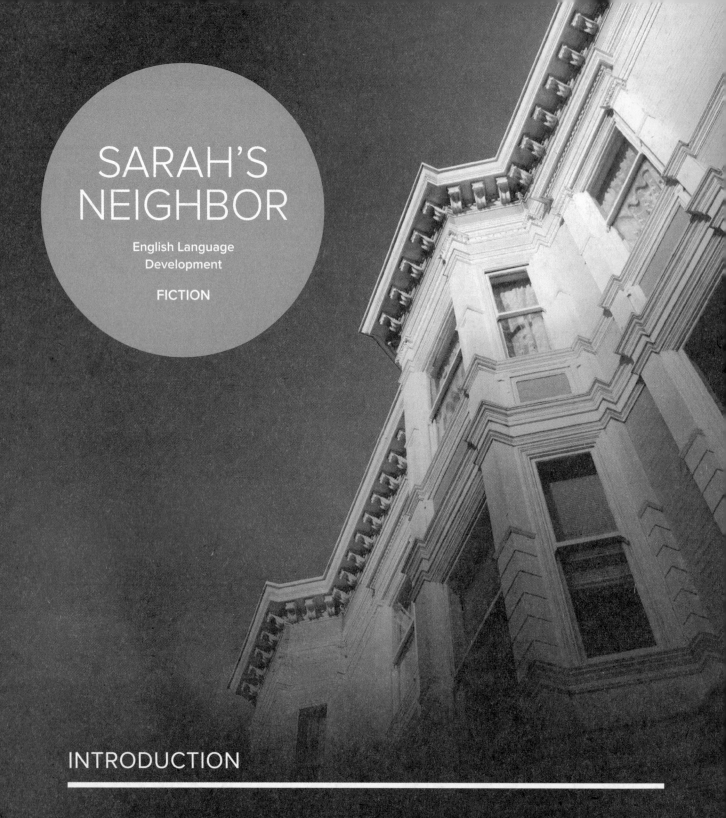

SARAH'S NEIGHBOR

English Language
Development

FICTION

INTRODUCTION

Set in San Francisco shortly after the bombing of Pearl Harbor during World War II, this short story focuses on a preteen girl's struggle to accept her parents' changing attitudes toward their Japanese neighbors, including her best friend, Ayako. As twelve year-old Sarah watches Ayako through the window, she longs to rekindle their friendship—but she is too scared of her father to disobey his orders.

"'That girl and her family are the enemy,' he'd said."

FIRST READ

1   Sarah looked through the kitchen window as she helped her mother do the dishes. Ayako, her neighbor and former best friend, sat on the swing set outside. She looked as lonely as a ghost. Nothing would have delighted Sarah more than dropping the silverware and **erupting** through the door to join Ayako, but she knew she couldn't. Her mind flashed to the conversation she had with her parents a few weeks ago, after the Japanese attacked Pearl Harbor.

2   Her father had just come home from an arduous shift at the San Francisco police department. People were angry about the bombing, he'd explained. There had been fighting in the streets. They couldn't trust the Japanese anymore—not even Ayako. He pulled out his sergeant's **badge** and started polishing it as a way of **accentuating** his **authority**. "That girl and her family are the enemy," he'd said.

3   Later, Sarah asked her mother to explain why she couldn't be friends with Ayako. It didn't make any sense. The bombing of Pearl Harbor was a serious attack. But Ayako hadn't been a part of it. Her mother **clasped** Sarah's hand. "Ayako didn't do anything bad. But she's a **symbol** of the people who did. The sergeant has given you your orders. It's best you follow them."

4   Sarah grabbed a plate to wash and focused on the circular movement of her own hands. She glued her eyes to the plate to take her mind off Ayako. There would be a harsh penalty for disobeying the sergeant's orders. She ached to ask her father for permission to go outside, but trepidation kept her mouth closed.

NOTES

5   The next morning, Sarah and her mother made a list of guests for her thirteenth birthday party. Her mother recited the names of each child from Sarah's class, and Sarah wrote them down. Then she had an idea. Tightening her grip on the pencil, she urgently sneaked another name into the middle of the list: Ayako's.

6   Without saying a word, she handed the list to her mother. At that moment, her father came in and began to scan the list over his wife's shoulder. When he got to Ayako's name, he practically **vibrated** with rage.

7   He faced Sarah and growled. "How many times have I told you that this girl cannot be your friend? I will not have my daughter spending time with someone like her! You will never see this girl again, or I will never see you again. Understand?"

8   Sarah opened her mouth. She wanted to stand up for herself. She wanted to tell her father that he was wrong, that Ayako is a good person. But all that came out was silence.

USING LANGUAGE   CA-CCSS: ELD.PI.8.6.c.Ex, ELD.PI.8.12.b.Ex

Read each word. Complete each row by filling in the correct root or affix meaning in the second column and definition in the third column.

Root/Affix Meaning Options		Definition Options
ardu- meaning "difficult" *-ous* meaning "full of"	*circ-* meaning "circle" *-ar* meaning "relating to"	relating to circles
		the state of feeling intense fear
sil- meaning "quiet" *-ence* meaning "the state of"	*trepid-* meaning "tremble" *-ation* meaning "the state of"	full of difficulty
		the state of being quiet
	pen- meaning "punish"	a punishment

Word	Root/Affix Meaning	Definition
arduous		
circular		
penalty		
trepidation		
silence		

MEANINGFUL INTERACTIONS CA-CCSS: ELD.PI.8.1.Ex

Work with your group to discuss your first impressions of the text. Take turns saying what you think about the characters and their situation. How would you describe the characters? How do the events in the story make you feel? Why do you think Sarah does not say anything to her father at the end of the story? Be sure to listen to your group members' ideas and wait your turn before speaking. Use the speaking frames to support your discussion. Last, use the self-assessment rubric to evaluate your participation in the discussion.

- In my opinion, Sarah / Sarah's mother / Sarah's father is . . . because . . .

- The events of the story make me feel . . . because . . .

- In my opinion, Sarah cannot speak because . . .

- I think you said . . . Why do you think that?

- I heard you say . . . , but . . . said . . .

- I agree with . . . because . . .

SELF-ASSESSMENT RUBRIC CA-CCSS: ELD.PI.8.1.Ex

	4 I did this well.	3 I did this pretty well.	2 I did this a little bit.	1 I did not do this.
I took an active part with others in doing the assigned task.				
I contributed effectively to the group's discussion.				
I waited my turn to speak.				
I listened carefully to my group members' ideas.				

REREAD

Reread paragraphs 1–3 of "Sarah's Neighbor." After you reread, complete the Using Language and Meaningful Interactions activities.

USING LANGUAGE CA-CCSS: ELD.PI.8.8.Ex

Read each quotation and note the word or phrase in bold. Then compare it to its synonym. Complete the chart by filling in the effect the bold word or phrase has on the sentence.

The bold word or phrase emphasizes... Options		
the sergeant's power over Sarah.	how isolated Ayako must feel.	the impact of the war.
the way the sergeant treats his family.	how restricted Sarah feels.	

Quotation	Synonym	The bold word or phrase emphasizes....
[Ayako] looked **as lonely as a ghost**.	alone	
Nothing would have delighted Sarah more than dropping the silverware and **erupting** through the door to join Ayako, but she knew she couldn't.	running	
He pulled out his sergeant's badge and started polishing it as a way of accentuating his **authority**.	job	
"That girl and her family are the **enemy**," he'd said.	opponent	
"The sergeant has given you your **orders**."	instructions	

MEANINGFUL INTERACTIONS   CA-CCSS: ELD.PI.8.1.Ex

Based on what you have read in "Sarah's Neighbor," what do you think about Sarah's relationship with each of her parents? What do you think about the characters' actions? Use the speaking frames below to ask and answer questions in small groups. Then, use the self-assessment rubric to evaluate your participation in the discussion.

- In my opinion, Sarah's relationship with her parents is . . . because . . .

- I think Sarah's relationship with her mother is . . . than her relationship with her father because . . .

- I think Sarah's choice to add Ayako's name to the list is . . . because . . .

- What should Sarah do when her father growls at her?

- I think Sarah should . . . because . . .

- Do you think Sarah should . . .

- I think this action is . . . because . . .

- I think you said . . . Why do you think that?

SELF-ASSESSMENT RUBRIC   CA-CCSS: ELD.PI.8.1.Ex

	4 I did this well.	3 I did this pretty well.	2 I did this a little bit.	1 I did not do this.
I took an active part with others in doing the assigned task.				
I contributed effectively to the group's discussion.				
I asked relevant questions.				
I answered questions clearly.				

REREAD

Reread paragraphs 4–8 of "Sarah's Neighbor." After you reread, complete the Using Language and Meaningful Interactions activities.

USING LANGUAGE CA-CCSS: ELD.PII.8.2.a.Ex

Read each sentence. Choose the noun each bold referring word or words refer to.

1. Sarah grabbed a plate to wash and focused on the circular movement of her own hands. **She** glued her eyes to the plate to take her mind off Ayako.

   ○ Sarah   ○ Ayako

2. There would be a harsh penalty for disobeying **the sergeant's** orders. She ached to ask her father for permission to go outside.

   ○ Sarah's father   ○ Sarah's mother

3. The next morning, Sarah and her mother made a list of guests for **her** thirteenth birthday party.

   ○ Sarah's mother   ○ Sarah

4. At that moment, her father came in and began to scan the list over **his wife's** shoulder.

   ○ Sarah   ○ Sarah's mother

5. He faced Sarah and growled. "How many times have I told you that **this girl** cannot be your friend?"

   ○ Ayako   ○ Sarah

6. **She** wanted to tell her father that he was wrong, that Ayako is a good person.

   ○ Sarah   ○ Ayako

MEANINGFUL INTERACTIONS CA-CCSS: ELD.PI.8.1.Ex

What do you think the theme of "Sarah's Neighbor" is? What key ideas from the text support that theme? Use the speaking frames to practice determining the theme and paraphrasing key ideas with a partner.

- In my opinion, the theme of the text is . . .

- One key idea from the text that supports this theme is . . .

- Another key idea that supports this theme is . . .

- These key ideas help me determine the theme because . . .

- I think you said the theme is . . . I agree / disagree because . . .

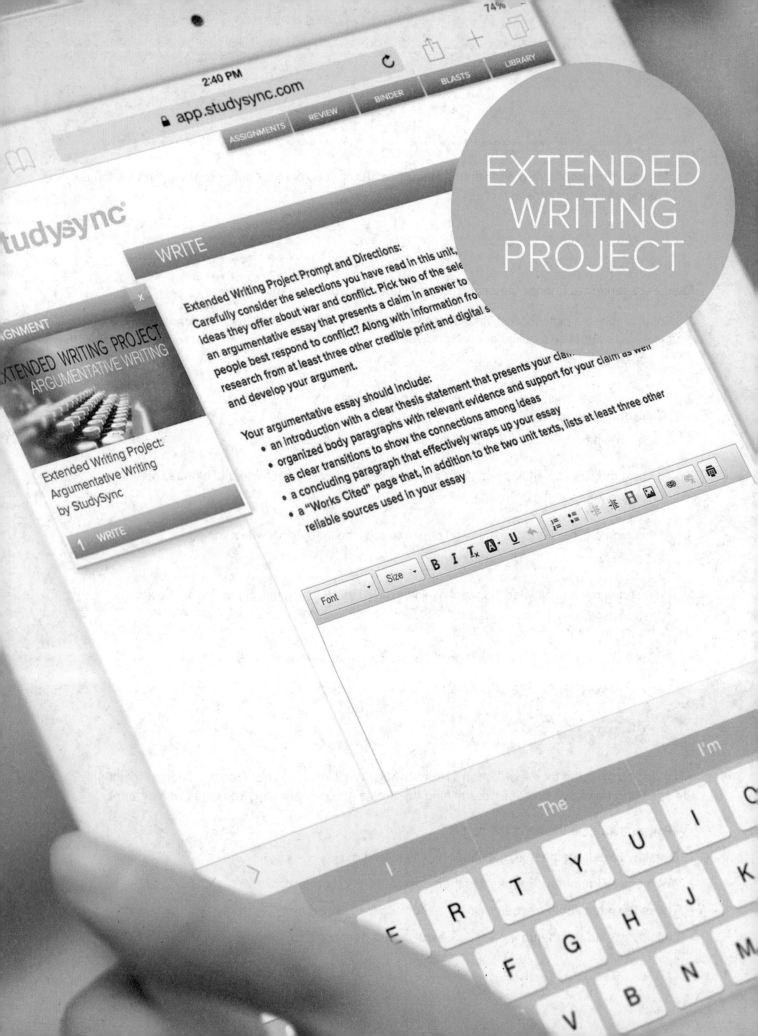

EXTENDED WRITING PROJECT

studysync®

WRITE

Extended Writing Project Prompt and Directions:

Carefully consider the selections you have read in this unit.
Ideas they offer about war and conflict. Pick two of the sele...
an argumentative essay that presents a claim in answer to...
people best respond to conflict? Along with information fro...
research from at least three other credible print and digital s...
and develop your argument.

Your argumentative essay should include:
- an introduction with a clear thesis statement that presents your cla...
- organized body paragraphs with relevant evidence and support for your claim as well
  as clear transitions to show the connections among ideas
- a concluding paragraph that effectively wraps up your essay
- a "Works Cited" page that, in addition to the two unit texts, lists at least three other
  reliable sources used in your essay

EXTENDED WRITING PROJECT
ARGUMENTATIVE WRITING

Extended Writing Project:
Argumentative Writing
by StudySync

1 WRITE

Font   Size   **B** *I* I_x A · U

ARGUMENTATIVE WRITING

WRITING PROMPT

Carefully consider the selections you have read in this unit, including their themes and the ideas they offer about war and conflict. Pick two of the selections from the unit and write an argumentative essay that presents a claim in answer to the following question: how can people best respond to conflict? Along with information from the selections, include research from at least three other credible print and digital sources to support your claim and develop your argument.

Your argumentative essay should include:

- An introduction with a clear thesis statement that presents your claim

- Organized body paragraphs with relevant evidence and support for your claim as well as clear transitions to show the connections among ideas

- A concluding paragraph that effectively wraps up your essay

- A Works Cited page that, in addition to the two unit texts, lists at least three other reliable sources used in your essay

Argumentative writing introduces a claim, or proposition, and supports it with clear evidence from a variety of relevant and reliable sources. It ends with a conclusion that sums up the arguments and evidence that supports the claim and restates the main idea. In this regard, writing an argument has much in common with other types of nonfiction writing. For example, it has a main idea, it presents supporting details related to the main idea, and it has the same physical structure with an introduction, body, and conclusion. The main difference between argumentative writing and other kinds of writing is its purpose. Argumentative writing is used to convince the audience that a claim is correct or valid. It can also be used to persuade readers that the author's

Please note that excerpts and passages in the StudySync® library and this workbook are intended as touchstones to generate interest in an author's work. The excerpts and passages do not substitute for the reading of entire texts, and StudySync® strongly recommends that students seek out and purchase the whole literary or informational work in order to experience it as the author intended. Links to online resellers are available in our digital library. In addition, complete works may be ordered through an authorized reseller by filling out and returning to StudySync® the order form enclosed in this workbook.

Reading & Writing Companion **83**

main idea is more valid than the ideas of others. This form of writing can be found in essays that offer opinions, such as editorials, letters to the editor in newspapers, debates, and similar texts. Features of argumentative writing include:

- Introduction with a clear claim or proposition, which can be thought of as a thesis statement
- A clear and logical organizational structure that includes an introduction, a body, and a conclusion
- Supporting details drawn from a combination of reliable, relevant sources
- Transitions that clearly show the relationships between ideas
- A formal style, achieved by precise language and domain-specific vocabulary
- Citations of sources and textual evidence to support claims
- A concluding paragraph that summarizes the proof that supports the thesis statement

As you continue with this extended writing project, you will receive additional instructions and practice to help you craft each of the elements of strong argumentative writing in your own essay.

 STUDENT MODEL

Before you begin writing your own argumentative essay, read this essay that one student wrote in response to the writing prompt. As you read this Student Model, make note of the features of argumentative writing listed above by highlighting and annotating the points and structures that the student used in his text.

Attitude: One Secret to Survival

For centuries, human beings have demonstrated countless ways to be cruel to other groups of people, especially during times of war. Entire ethnic groups have been targeted for the simple reason that they were born into the "wrong" culture or family. Enslavement, imprisonment, and even wholesale slaughter of people who were thought to be "different" have put black marks on the histories of many countries. This mistreatment by people in authority can damage its victims, even if they survive physically. Yet there are individuals who manage to come through their ordeal and heal. There are also people who, even though they did not survive, continue to inspire us to this day with stories of their courage.

One well-known example of such inspiration comes from *Anne Frank, in Anne Frank: The Diary of a Young Girl.* This young girl has inspired millions with her firsthand account of life for her and her Jewish family as they hid from the Nazis in Amsterdam. Other inspiring stories come from the real-life letters of children in the United States' internment camps for Japanese Americans during World War II. Some of these letters were collected in the book *Dear Miss Breed: True Stories of the Japanese American Incarceration During World War II and a Librarian Who Made a Difference* by Joanne Oppenheim. This book, along with *Anne Frank: The Diary of a Young Girl,* explain the situations these families underwent, but they also show one path to graceful endurance: a positive attitude. Coping with impossible situations, such as living in hiding from the Nazis or enduring the Japanese internment camps, took a certain kind of strength, along with a positive attitude. As these works show, positive thinking is one of the best ways to respond to conflict, as well as an effective path to healing for those who survive physical abuse or hardship at the hands of others.

The impact of a positive attitude is shown in the thoughts and words of real people. In *Anne Frank: The Diary of a Young Girl,* Anne's accounts reveal a positive attitude that later served as inspiration for millions of people. For example, in her diary entry dated Saturday, July 11, 1942, even while living in crowded, difficult conditions while hiding from the Nazis—worried that the entire family might be discovered at any time—Anne notes that "Thanks to Father—who brought my entire postcard and movie-star collection here beforehand—and to a brush and a pot of glue, I was able to plaster the wall with pictures. It looks much more cheerful" (Frank 20). She also writes of the everyday details of her life, such as the chiming of the clock near their hidden location. A similar example from a different situation comes from a Japanese internment camp in the United States from the same period. In *Dear Miss Breed: True Stories of the Japanese American Incarceration During World War II and a Librarian Who Made a Difference,* Louise Ogawa writes to Miss Breed about the beauty of the Colorado River they had crossed on their way to the incarceration camp. Louise showed that she was trying to find positive things to think about when she wrote, "Yesterday, I ate rice, weenies, and cabbage with a knife. That was a new experience for me!" (Oppenheim 114). These two individuals show that they were trying to keep a positive attitude in extremely difficult circumstances. Although some may argue that a positive attitude didn't really help Anne Frank, who ended up dying in the Bergen-Belsen concentration camp, her strength and spirit while enduring tremendously difficult

Please note that excerpts and passages in the StudySync® library and this workbook are intended as touchstones to generate interest in an author's work. The excerpts and passages do not substitute for the reading of entire texts, and StudySync® strongly recommends that students seek out and purchase the whole literary or informational work in order to experience it as the author intended. Links to online resellers are available in our digital library. In addition, complete works may be ordered through an authorized reseller by filling out and returning to StudySync® the order form enclosed in this workbook.

Reading & Writing Companion   **85**

circumstances have inspired countless individuals across the decades. The diary has been translated into 70 languages, and over 28 million people have visited her home since it opened as a museum in 1960 (The Anne Frank House). Her positive attitude therefore has had a profound impact beyond her own life and cannot be discounted.

More evidence about the effects of a positive attitude can be found in the writings of certain scholars. Some of them have studied how people react to hardships that are created by other human beings. An article from the Florida Center for Instructional Technology talks about different types of music that was created during the Holocaust as the Jewish people struggled to survive. So many resistance songs were written at the time, according to the article, that composers simply couldn't create enough tunes. This forced people to recycle existing music with the new words that expressed the things they were feeling (The Florida Center for Instructional Technology 1). One line from a play of the time has a child in a Warsaw ghetto orphanage crying, "I cannot sing . . . I'm so hungry." A caretaker replies, "We all are! That is why we must sing" (The Florida Center for Instructional Technology 1). Caroline Schaumann of Emory University argues that "Remaining mentally engaged in the world, whether the greater one beyond the physical barriers imposed by the Nazis or the lesser one inside the camps, was another significant aid to survival" (Schaumann 9). Obviously, attitude plays a key role in surviving such situations.

Psychologists also agree that the mental attitude of individuals in these horrible situations is very important. Karen Lawson, MD, states that ". . . positive emotions literally reverse the physical effects of negativity and build up psychological resources that contribute to a flourishing life" (Lawson 2). In one study cited by Lawson, people who focused on gratitude felt happier, slept better, and had fewer physical problems than those who did not. She also notes that strong people have the ability to maintain positive feelings while enduring extremely negative circumstances, allowing them to overcome some of the negative impacts of their situations (Lawson 2). She concludes that people who focus on the positive routinely become stronger in the face of crisis (Lawson 3). This shows that positive attitudes must have helped some people face these dire situations with such courage that we remember them today.

Attitude, then, is not only important in our day-to-day lives. It is also necessary for survival in situations where life has been turned upside down by outside forces, and even in circumstances when safety is threatened. Positive attitude contributes to the psychological strength that helps victims of even horrible situations like the Holocaust and the internment camps continue to survive under extremely harsh conditions. These thought patterns continue to serve victims of trauma after they are returned to safety. It can contribute to their healing. The stories told in *Anne Frank: The Diary of a Young Girl* and in *Dear Miss Breed: True Stories of the Japanese American Incarceration During World War II and a Librarian Who Made a Difference* show the importance of such an attitude and the inspiration that people such as Anne Frank and Louise Ogawa provide. Positive attitudes contribute to the mental and emotional strength that is necessary to survive physical abuse or hardship at the hands of others.

Works Cited

Frank, Anne. *Anne Frank: The Diary of a Young Girl.* New York: Doubleday, 1952.

Lawson, Karen, M.D. "How Do Thoughts & Emotions Impact Health?" *Taking Charge of Your Health and Well-Being.* University of Minnesota. Web. 12 Dec. 2014. http://www.takingcharge.csh.umn.edu/enhance-your-wellbeing/health/thoughts-emotions/how-do-thoughts-emotions-impact-health

"Music of the Ghettos and Camps." *A Teacher's Guide to the Holocaust.* The Florida Center for Instructional Technology, College of Education, University of South Florida. C. 1997–2013. Web. 12 Dec. 2014. http://fcit.coedu.usf.edu/holocaust/arts/musVicti.htm

Oppenheim, Joanne. *Dear Miss Breed: True Stories of the Japanese American Incarceration During World War II and a Librarian Who Made a Difference.* New York: Scholastic, Inc., 2006.

Schaumann, Caroline. "Factors Influencing Survival During the Holocaust." *History in Dispute, Vol. 11: The Holocaust, 1933–1945.* Benjamin Frankel, ed. St. James Press, 1999. Web. 12 December 2014. 1999. Web. 12 December 2014. http://www.google.com/url?sa=t&rct=j&q=&esrc=s&source=web&cd=1&ved=0CCMQFjAA&url=http%3A%2F%2Ffacweb.northseattle.edu%2Fcadler%2FGlobal_Dialogues%2FReadings%2FMaus_Readings%2FFactors%2520Influencing%2520Survival%2520during%2520the%2520Holocaust.

doc&ei=YT-LVKuOKYqOyQSCpoCoDQ&usg=AFQjCNEoEdrB6D18vVuQyPy96
REwrVu1mQ&sig2=Ui_cnN68CkQxmdGvtLNPWA&bvm=bv.81828268,d.aWw&
cad=rja

Virtual Museum of The Anne Frank House. Anne Frank Stichting. 28 April 2010.
Web. 27 March 2015. http://www.annefrank.org/en/subsites/timeline/postwar-
period-1945—present-day/the-diary-is-published/1950/the-diary-of-anne-
frank-is-published-in-germany-in-an-edition-of-4500-copies-a-very-
successful-paperback-edition-follows-in-1955/#!/en/subsites/timeline/
postwar-period-1945—present-day/the-diary-is-published/1950/the-diary-
of-anne-frank-is-published-in-germany-in-an-edition-of-4500-copies-a-very-
successful-paperback-edition-follows-in-1955/

http://www.annefrank.org/en/News/Press/Visitor-numbers/

THINK QUESTIONS

1. What is the claim in this essay, and where does it appear?

2. What support does the writer provide to convince her audience that her claim is valid?

3. How does the writer give proper credit to her sources?

4. As you consider the writing prompt, which selections or other resources do you plan to use to write your own argumentative essay? What are some ideas that you may want to develop in your own piece?

5. Based on what you have read, listened to, or researched, how would you respond to the question: *What does our response to conflict say about us?*

NOTES

PREWRITE

CA-CCSS: CA.RI.8.1, CA.RI.8.2, CA.RI.8.3, CA.W.8.1a, CA.W.8.5, CA.W.8.6, CA.W.8.9b, CA.SL.8.1a

WRITING PROMPT

Carefully consider the selections you have read in this unit, including their themes and the ideas they offer about war and conflict. Pick two of the selections from the unit and write an argumentative essay that presents a claim in answer to the following question: how can people best respond to conflict? Along with information from the selections, include research from at least three other credible print and digital sources to support your claim and develop your argument.

Your argumentative essay should include:

- An introduction with a clear thesis statement that presents your claim
- Organized body paragraphs with relevant evidence and support for your claim as well as clear transitions to show the connections among ideas
- A concluding paragraph that effectively wraps up your essay
- A Works Cited page that, in addition to the two unit texts, lists at least three other reliable sources used in your essay

In addition to studying techniques authors use to present information, you have been reading and learning about stories that feature firsthand accounts of people who lived through times of conflict. In this Extended Writing Project, you will use argumentative writing techniques to compose your own argumentative essay about how people can best respond to conflict.

Since the topic of your argumentative essay will have to do with how people can best respond to conflicts, you will want to think about how the people you've read about handled the situations in which they found themselves. Consider the following questions:

- What harsh situation or conflict did the people in the text face?
- How did this situation affect their daily lives?
- What specific behaviors and attitudes characterized their response to the situation?
- What impact did their response to the situation have on them?
- What ideas does the text suggest about how people can best respond to conflict?

Make a list of the answers to these questions and any others you think of for at least two different texts from this unit. As you note your ideas, do you see any patterns or commonalities? Are there ideas that are repeated? Remember that you will be designing a claim and then supporting it with evidence from the texts you've read in this unit and from your own research. Looking for patterns and thoughts that can be thoroughly supported will help you solidify the ideas that you want to address in your essay. Use this model to get started with your own prewriting:

Text: *Anne Frank: The Diary of a Young Girl* by Anne Frank
Conflict: Anne and her family were in danger from the Nazis during World War II. The Franks were Jewish, and the Nazis were sending Jewish people to concentration camps, where they were either killed upon arrival or worked to death.
What Happened: Anne and her family went into hiding in the home of a friend. They were uprooted from their own house, had little contact with others, and lived in cramped, crowded rooms. Anne's diary is a record of the many things she did to make the best of a bad situation, such as pasting cheerful postcards on the wall and attempting to view the experience as a kind of "vacation." These details reveal her positive attitude, which likely made the ordeal easier for her to bear.

SKILL: RESEARCH AND NOTE-TAKING

 ## DEFINE

Several types of writing require authors to conduct research in order to find evidence to support their thesis or claim. **Research** is the process of asking questions about a topic and finding answers from multiple sources in print or online. Consider your topic and claim. Then ask yourself at least two or three questions whose answers will help you prove your point. Examine other articles, websites, books, speeches, or other related information to gather answers to your research questions. If you find too much information, and you're overwhelmed, you should consider narrowing your questions and making them more specific. If, on the other hand, you have difficulty finding enough sources to examine, you may need to broaden your research questions. In other words, your questions should guide your research, and your research results will lead you to refine your questions.

As you research to find support for your claim, you will need to consult multiple sources. **Sources** are the articles, documents, websites, books, or other information that an author uses to gather information about his or her topic. It is important to use only reliable sources. **Reliable sources** are those that provide accurate, trustworthy, and unbiased information about the topic. Examples of reliable sources include websites from the government or from academic institutions. Articles or books written by experts in the field, or firsthand accounts of events written by people who were present at the time (primary sources) are also reliable sources. Some types of sources are noted for being unreliable, and should not be used for academic writing. These include personal websites, blogs, advertisements, commercial literature (.com websites), and social media posts. These are not considered reliable because they contain personal opinions. The authors are also likely to have an agenda that may not include an honest or balanced presentation of facts.

As you explore the sources of information for your research, you will need to write down some of the information that you find. **Note-taking** is writing down the answers to your research questions as well as any other information that seems important about your topic or claim. It is also important when taking notes that you write down the details that identify the source. This includes the names of the authors, the title, and the publisher. If you copy words, phrases, or sentences directly, be sure to note where they came from within the document so you can give proper credit in your essay. If you do not write down direct quotations, be sure you have accurately paraphrased the author's ideas so you do not accidentally plagiarize the work of others. When you paraphrase, you express the meaning of something written or spoken using different words. But be careful. You do not want to misrepresent an author's ideas by paraphrasing them too broadly. At the same time, you need to change more than a word or two when you paraphrase.

 ## IDENTIFICATION AND APPLICATION

- Writers begin research by framing one, two, or more questions related to their topic and claim. These will guide research by providing a focus that the writer can search for.

- Research is a cycle in which you create a few questions, look for sources of related information, and then refine the questions and search again. There are several reasons to refine search questions:

  › Finding too much information means that the questions are too broad. Writers should make the questions more specific or eliminate some questions if too much information in too many sources is found.

  › Finding too little information or too few sources means that questions may be too narrowly focused. Change the questions to be more general or add more questions to the search.

  › Writers should keep in mind that more specific search terms will narrow their search results. For example, "Women in the Civil War" will likely lead to fewer but more specific results than "the Civil War."

  › Writers have several tools available for searching. In addition to search engines, other resources include scholarly databases, libraries, interviews with experts, museum collections, and so forth.

- Just as writers should use multiple tools for searching, they should also plan to consult a wide variety of sources as they research.

  › These can include (but are not limited to) print sources; audio-visual sources such as documentaries, podcasts, photographs, or films; and electronic sources such as websites, articles, speeches and interviews.

- Primary sources come directly from people who experienced an event. This can include letters, photographs, diaries or journals, official documents, autobiographies, and interviews. These sources can often provide very convincing evidence.

NOTES

- Secondary sources generally include written interpretation and analysis of primary source materials. Secondary sources include articles from encyclopedias, textbooks or histories, news analyses, or documentaries about the topic. These sources can also provide useful information.

- It is important for writers of argumentative essays to use reliable sources only. The sources should be accurate and unbiased. Reliable sources include information from experts respected in the field, researchers, academic programs, or the government.

  › Writers should evaluate online sources based on the ending of the URL or web address. URLs that contain ".gov" are typically maintained by government agencies. Those that contain ".edu" are run by academic institutions such as universities or schools. Those that contain ".org" addresses are typically operated by museums or other non-profit agencies. All of these are likely to supply accurate information to support claims.

  › Other sources of reliable information include online news agencies or respected print publishers.

- The writer should think about and evaluate each source. Make sure it is accurate, related to the topic, and appropriate for your audience.

- Writers need to take many notes while doing research. It is important to keep these notes well-organized. The following strategies help writers take notes. They will be useful when writing an argumentative essay:

  › Put information about references on cards: Whether a writer chooses to use paper note cards or a computer system that serves the same purpose, note cards are very important. Writers must write down all of the information about the source that will later be needed for citations and a bibliography, which is an organized list of sources. This includes the author's name, title of the work, publisher, city and state of publication, date of publication, and the page numbers referenced. Note the date of access if the source is electronic.

  › Use a separate card for each fact, idea, observation, quotation, or other information found while you research. Code the cards with a letter or number that matches the source card where the information came from. Clearly mark quotations and note who to credit. If an item is not a direct quotation, be sure you have paraphrased accurately and avoided plagiarism, or copying another person's work.

MODEL

The writer of the Student Model essay "Attitude: One Secret to Survival" supported her claim by finding textual evidence in two texts located during

NOTES

the research process. Her research note cards from the two texts are reproduced below:

Bibliography Card: Source 1

Article: "Music of the Ghettos and Camps"

Publication: *A Teacher's Guide to the Holocaust*

Publication date: 1952

Publisher: The Florida Center for Technology, College of Education, University of South Florida

Date: 1997–2013

Media: Web

Accessed: 12 Dec. 2014

Bibliography Card: Source 2

Article: "How Do Thoughts & Emotions Impact Health?"

Publication: *Taking Charge of Your Health and Well-Being*

Author: Karen Lawson, M.D.

Publication date: 18 August 2013

Publisher: University of Minnesota

Media: Web

Accessed: 12 Dec. 2014

Holocaust: Songs

Source 1

Songs showed will to survive

Attitude and Health:

Source 2

"Resilient people are able to experience tough emotions like pain, sorrow, frustration, and grief without falling apart—in fact, some people are able to look at challenging times with optimism and hope, knowing that their hardships will lead to personal growth and an expanded outlook on life."

Holocaust: Positive Attitude

Source 1

"Laughter became a necessity..."

Attitude and Health:

Source 2

"Positive emotions have a scientific purpose—to help the body recover from the ill effects of negative emotions."

NOTES

Holocaust: Songs
Source 1

"A majority of ghetto street songs were sung to pre-existing melodies, a technique known as 'contra fact.' Contra fact became necessary because composers couldn't generate new music fast enough for all 'f the lyrics being written."

Attitude and Health:
Source 2

"These positive emotions literally reverse the physical effects of negativity and build up psychological resources that contribute to a flourishing life."

Holocaust: Other Arts
Source 1

"A majority of ghetto street songs were sung to pre-existing melodies, a technique known as contra fact. Contra fact became necessary because composers couldn't generate new music fast enough for all of the lyrics being written."

Attitude and Health:
Source 2

Benefits of gratitude include good sleep, happier outlook, and fewer physical problems.

The author used two types of cards in her research: bibliography cards and note cards. The bibliography cards record all of the information necessary for the Works Cited page that should be placed at the end of the essay. The note cards each contain separate ideas from the sources that are clearly marked. They show where the ideas or information come from. Information that was taken directly from the source is recorded in quotes. If the sources had been print, each card would also have included a page number where the information was found. Organizing the note cards in this way saved the author a lot of time and energy when writing. The information for citations and the Works Cited page was readily available, so she did not have to retrace her research steps when she decided to use a piece of information that needed to be credited, and she was positive as to which bits of information were direct quotes and which were paraphrases.

By putting a subject on top, a code to connect the card with the matching source, and one fact, quote, idea, example, or definition on each card, the author made it much easier to organize her notes later when she was writing. Using this identification system, she could shuffle the note cards into any order and still connect the idea with the proper source.

Please note that excerpts and passages in the StudySync® library and this workbook are intended as touchstones to generate interest in an author's work. The excerpts and passages do not substitute for the reading of entire texts, and StudySync® strongly recommends that students seek out and purchase the whole literary or informational work in order to experience it as the author intended. Links to online resellers are available in our digital library. In addition, complete works may be ordered through an authorized reseller by filling out and returning to StudySync® the order form enclosed in this workbook.

Reading & Writing Companion   **95**

Now, let's look at how this writer used some of her research notes to write the following excerpt from "Attitude: One Secret to Survival":

> Psychologists also agree that the mental attitude of individuals in these situations is important. **Karen Lawson, MD, states that ". . . positive emotions literally reverse the physical effects of negativity and build up psychological resources that contribute to a flourishing life" (Lawson 2).** In one study cited by Lawson, people who focused themselves on gratitude felt happier, slept better, and had fewer physical problems than those who did not. She also notes that resilient people have the ability to experience very negative circumstances while retaining positive feelings, allowing them to overcome some of the negative impacts of their situation (Lawson 2).

Examine the bold print in the paragraph. The writer used the information from "How Do Thoughts & Emotions Impact Health?" in *Taking Charge of Your Health and Well-Being* to begin to build a case for her claim that positive attitude contributes to survival. The pieces of information that she included begin to build a case for the idea that people try to stay positive in such circumstances. Let's look at the note card where this quotation came from again.

Attitude and Health:

Source 2

"These positive emotions literally reverse the physical effects of negativity and build up psychological resources that contribute to a flourishing life."

We can see that this direct quote came from Source 2.

 PRACTICE

Now it's your turn. Review the information you noted during the Prewrite lesson. Get some note cards or set up a digital note-card system on a computer, and complete the following tasks:

- Find at least three other reliable, relevant sources suitable for your topic.
- Create bibliography cards for these additional sources and label or code them so you can connect note cards to them.
- Make at least six note cards that contain pieces of evidence about your topic. These can be quotations, ideas, facts, statistics, or other pieces of

information. Make sure they are connected to what you plan to write in response to the prompt. Be sure to label each note card with the code for the matching bibliography card.

After you have found at least three additional sources and created at least six note cards, trade information with a peer for some feedback. Give your peer the prewriting information as well as at least two bibliography cards and at least six note cards with one piece of information on each. Review your peer's work while yours is being reviewed. Consider the following questions:

- Why are these additional sources considered to be reliable? How are they connected to the topic?
- How do these research card notes relate to the information from the prewriting exercise? In what way is the information from all the sources connected?
- If you were to read the paper written from these research notes, what questions would you still have about this topic?
- What suggestions can you make to your peer to improve his or her research?

Remember that suggestions will be most helpful if they are positive and specific. Be kind and polite as you review your peer's work.

SKILL:
THESIS
STATEMENT

 DEFINE

In argumentative writing, the thesis statement is the claim that the author makes in the introduction and then proves in the body of the essay with reasons and evidence. It is the most important sentence in the entire essay because it is the focal point. It expresses the author's main idea and tells the reader what position the author is taking on a debatable topic. The claim, or thesis statement, appears in the introductory paragraph and is often the last sentence in the paragraph. The body of the essay provides reasons in support of the author's claim and offers details such as facts, examples, quotations, or other evidence that the claim is correct.

 IDENTIFICATION AND APPLICATION

A thesis statement (or claim)

- takes a clear stand on an issue.
- lets the reader know what the author supports.
- responds fully and completely to an essay prompt.
- is presented in the introduction paragraph.

 MODEL

Reread the introduction paragraph from the Student Model essay, "Attitude: One Secret to Survival":

> For centuries, human beings have demonstrated countless ways to be cruel to other groups of people, especially during times of war. Entire ethnic groups have been targeted for the simple reason that they were born into the "wrong" culture or family. Enslavement, imprisonment, and even wholesale

slaughter of people who were thought to be "different" have put black marks on the histories of many countries. This mistreatment by people in authority can damage its victims, even if they survive physically. Yet there are individuals who manage to come through their ordeal and heal. There are also people who, even though they did not survive, continue to inspire us to this day with stories of their courage. One well-known example of such inspiration comes from Anne Frank, in *Anne Frank: The Diary of a Young Girl.* This young girl has inspired millions with her firsthand account of life for her and her Jewish family as they hid from the Nazis in Amsterdam. Other inspiring stories come from the real-life letters of children in the United States' internment camps for Japanese Americans during World War II. Some of these letters were collected in the book, *Dear Miss Breed: True Stories of the Japanese American Incarceration During World War II and a Librarian Who Made a Difference* by Joanne Oppenheim. This book, along with *Anne Frank: The Diary of a Young Girl,* explain the situations these families underwent, but they also show one path to graceful endurance: a positive attitude. Coping with impossible situations, such as living in hiding from the Nazis or enduring the Japanese internment camps, took a certain kind of strength, along with a positive attitude. **As these works show, positive thinking is one of the best ways to respond to conflict, as well as an effective path to healing for those who survive physical abuse or hardship at the hands of others.**

The bold-faced sentence is the thesis statement, or claim. This student's thesis statement responds to the prompt by presenting a claim about how people can respond effectively to conflict. It reminds readers that the author believes a positive attitude is critical to survival in extreme and abusive circumstances.

 ## PRACTICE

Now it's your turn. Craft a thesis statement, or claim, for your argumentative essay that clearly answers the question: "How can people best respond to conflict?" Your thesis should clearly articulate your central idea as well as your opinion about it. When you have written your thesis statement, exchange with a partner and critique one another's work. How clear is the author's central idea? How does the thesis statement relate to the prompt? Does the author take a clear stand or express a clear opinion? Offer suggestions to one another, and remember to be kind and constructive when you discuss each other's work.

Please note that excerpts and passages in the StudySync® library and this workbook are intended as touchstones to generate interest in an author's work. The excerpts and passages do not substitute for the reading of entire texts, and StudySync® strongly recommends that students seek out and purchase the whole literary or informational work in order to experience it as the author intended. Links to online resellers are available in our digital library. In addition, complete works may be ordered through an authorized reseller by filling out and returning to StudySync® the order form enclosed in this workbook.

Reading & Writing
Companion

99

Copyright © BookheadEd Learning, LLC

SKILL:
ORGANIZE
ARGUMENTATIVE
WRITING

DEFINE

The purpose of argumentative writing is to convince readers to adopt a particular point of view on an issue, to take action, or to choose a side. To do this, writers must **organize** and present the case to support their **thesis,** or claim. They must give reasons the reader should agree with their view and then support those reasons with **evidence.** Evidence consists of ideas, facts, details, definitions, examples, and other information from other sources. This information is presented in a logical manner so that one idea naturally leads to the next. The purpose of writing an argument is to inform and persuade readers.

Writers of argumentative essays use an **organizational structure** that is appropriate, or correct, for their topic and its support. The essay is structured with an introduction that contains the thesis statement, **body paragraphs** that identify and explain the reasons and evidence that support the claim, and a conclusion that often includes a summary of the evidence and perhaps a call to action. Writers usually use a graphic organizer, **outline,** or other method for arranging their material. This helps them organize their ideas to express them effectively.

IDENTIFICATION AND APPLICATION

- The introduction, or first paragraph of an argumentative essay, uses a "hook" to grab the reader's attention. A "hook" is an opening statement that will make it almost impossible for a reader to put down your essay. It may contain a fascinating fact or statistic. A good quotation is also an excellent way to attract your reader, as it connects the essay to a point in history. The first paragraph then introduces the issue and the main sources of information. It ends with a clear claim about the issue or thesis statement.

- The body paragraphs of the argumentative essay are built around the author's claims and the reasons that will convince the reader that the claim is correct. Each paragraph should focus on one claim, the reason for it, and its supporting evidence. Writers might consider:

> › The reasons they wish to use to show the claim is correct. These should be presented in a logical order, such as least important to most important, most general to most specific, or less common to more common.
> › The evidence from the sources that supports the claim. Each piece of evidence should clearly relate to the reason that is the topic of the paragraph. Each should add support that leads the reader to conclude that the claim is correct.

- The argumentative essay ends with a conclusion that summarizes the most important points. It clearly shows the logical path between the issue and proof that the claim is correct.

- Effective transitions create connections and make clear the relationships you find between reasons and the evidence in different sources. One idea should lead naturally to the next. The reader should be able to take small, logical steps through the essay and end up concluding that the writer's claim is correct. Some transitions to consider include:

> › Sequential order: *first, next, then, finally, last, initially, ultimately*
> › Cause and effect: *because, accordingly, as a result, effect, so*
> › Compare and contrast: *like, unlike, also, both, similarly* or *similar, although, while, but, however*
> › Problem and solution: *so, as a result, consequently, therefore*

 ## MODEL

Writing a good argumentative essay is much like building a house. A builder needs to start with a good, solid foundation just like a writer needs a good, solid thesis statement. A builder needs to use strong wooden boards to build the walls and the roof, just like a writer must use solid reasons in the right places to build the body of the essay. A builder puts the strong boards together with nails, and a writer nails the reasons together with evidence.

The writer of the Student Model argumentative essay focused on answering the following question in the prompt: How can people best respond to conflict? She chose two example texts about people who lived through horrible abuse in the concentration camps and in the internment camps and found a commonality: the people who survived and those who are considered to be inspirational worked to keep a positive attitude in terrible situations. The sources that the author found in her research confirm this claim.

Please note that excerpts and passages in the StudySync® library and this workbook are intended as touchstones to generate interest in an author's work. The excerpts and passages do not substitute for the reading of entire texts, and StudySync® strongly recommends that students seek out and purchase the whole literary or informational work in order to experience it as the author intended. Links to online resellers are available in our digital library. In addition, complete works may be ordered through an authorized reseller by filling out and returning to StudySync® the order form enclosed in this workbook.

Reading & Writing Companion **101**

The writer of the Student Model essay developed three reasons to prove that a positive attitude is one of the best ways to respond to conflict. The second paragraph, which has the topic sentence **"The impact of a positive attitude is shown in the thoughts and words of real people,"** allowed her to pull examples from primary sources to prove her point. The third body paragraph, which has the topic sentence of **"More evidence about the effects of a positive attitude can be found in the writings of certain scholars,"** enabled the writer to provide additional evidence from scholarly sources of the importance of a positive attitude. The fourth body paragraph, which has the topic sentence **"Psychologists also agree that the mental attitude of individuals in these horrible situations is very important,"** allowed the writer to introduce the opinions of medical experts to prove the claim. So the writer built her claim by moving from accounts in literature to commentary from scholars and teachers to expert testimony about the matter.

The writer of the Student Model argumentative essay, "Attitude: One Secret to Survival," knew that she had to give the proof for her claim in a logical fashion, and so she used a graphic organizer to sort through the ideas and put them in order. Remember that all notes should come from specific sources.

Claim: Positive thinking is one of the best ways to respond to conflict, as well as an effective path to healing for those who survive physical abuse or hardship at the hands of others.		
The impact of a positive attitude is shown in the thoughts and words of real people.	More evidence about the effects of a positive attitude can be found in the writings of certain scholars.	Psychologists also agree that the mental attitude of individuals in these horrible situations is very important.

Firsthand accounts from those who experienced conflict demonstrate the benefits of positive thinking.	Scholar's Observation: So many song lyrics were written during the Holocaust that composers couldn't write enough music for them. (FCIT, online article)	Psychologist's conclusion: Positive attitude increased strength, and strength increased positive attitude. (Lawson, online article)
Firsthand Observation: Anne Frank had cheerful pictures on her wall. (*Anne Frank: The Diary of a Young Girl*)	Scholar's Observation: Line from a play: "So hungry I cannot sing / That is why we must sing" (FCIT, online article)	Psychologist's conclusion: Gratitude improved sleep and health. (Lawson, online article)
Firsthand Observation: Anne Frank noticed the chiming of the clock. (*Anne Frank: The Diary of a Young Girl*)	Scholar's Observation: Mental engagement impacted victims' survival. (Schaumann, online article)	Psychologist's conclusion: Positive attitude reversed some physical problems. (Lawson, online article)
Firsthand Observation: Louise Ogawa enjoyed learning how to eat weenies and cabbage with a knife. (*Dear Miss Breed*)		
Firsthand Observation: Louise Ogawa noticed the beautiful scenery of the Colorado River. (*Dear Miss Breed*)		

PRACTICE

Complete the StudySync *Organize Argumentative Writing Three-Column Chart* graphic organizer by filling in the information you gathered in the Prewrite and Research and Note-Taking stages of writing your essay, as well as any additional information you have gathered since then. You may choose to organize the chart according to three reasons in support of your claim, three types of support for your claim, or some other system of your choosing. Please include specific sources of information. When you are finished, trade with a partner and offer each other feedback. How well has the writer organized his or her ideas? Has the writer noted any differences between specific ideas? Does the organization of ideas make sense? Can you offer any suggestions for improvement? Remember to be considerate and respectful as you offer constructive suggestions to one another.

SKILL:
SUPPORTING
DETAILS

⭐ DEFINE

Writers of argumentative essays support their claim (or thesis) with relevant evidence called supporting details. These are pieces of information that help the reader understand the topic. The information comes from credible, or trustworthy sources. The author uses logical reasoning to connect these pieces of information. In this way, the author builds a solid case for the claim made in the introduction. The purpose is to persuade the reader to share the same view and perhaps take action related to the issue.

IDENTIFICATION AND APPLICATION

The supporting details, or **evidence,** form the most important part of the argument and should include some of the following:

- Facts important to understanding the topic
- Examples that highlight the topic
- Research related to the main idea or thesis
- Quotations from experts, eyewitnesses, or other source material
- Conclusions of scientific findings and studies
- Definitions from reference material

As the writer does research to find supporting details, he or she should evaluate each detail to make sure it truly supports the claim. It can also lead to a new understanding of a topic or help the reader make logical connections between the evidence and the claim. Evidence, or supporting details, can come from many sources, including encyclopedias, online sources, research papers, newspaper articles, graphs and charts, critical reviews, documentaries, firsthand accounts, biographies, and more.

Please note that excerpts and passages in the StudySync® library and this workbook are intended as touchstones to generate interest in an author's work. The excerpts and passages do not substitute for the reading of entire texts, and StudySync® strongly recommends that students seek out and purchase the whole literary or informational work in order to experience it as the author intended. Links to online resellers are available in our digital library. In addition, complete works may be ordered through an authorized reseller by filling out and returning to StudySync® the order form enclosed in this workbook.

Reading & Writing Companion   105

MODEL

Let's examine the Counterpoint essay, "The Dangers of Fictionalizing History," in *Teaching History Through Fiction*. The Counterpoint writer begins his essay by stating his claim: "Teaching history through the use of fiction, including stories, novels, and films, is often misleading and can be dangerous, and John Boyne's *The Boy in the Striped Pajamas* shows why." In the first body paragraph of the essay, the Counterpoint writer quotes the same passage from children's book author Valerie Tripp that was used to support the claim in the Point essay: "Fiction can make history matter—make it irresistible—to young readers." But he then offers additional insight to show why Tripp's thoughts on the issue are actually more supportive of his own:

> No one would consider Valerie Tripp an opponent of using fiction to teach history. **On the teachinghistory.org website, Tripp notes that "fiction can make history matter—make it irresistible—to young readers" (Tripp, "Vitamins in Chocolate Cake"). Yet Tripp, an author of youth fiction herself, also knows the dangers.** She offers this warning to teachers: "When choosing historical fiction to use in the classroom as a way to interest students in history, I'd say: First, do no harm. That is, before it is used in a history classroom, historical fiction should be checked for bias, for anachronistic voice and views, and for shying away from honest presentation of the period. What is not said is as misleading as what is said!" (Tripp, "Neither Spinach Nor Potato Chip").

> **Judged according to Tripp's criteria, teachers should use *The Boy in the Striped Pajamas* with caution. Boyne's bias rests not in his personal beliefs about the Holocaust, but in his view of storytelling.**

Boyne's view of storytelling, which the Counterpoint writer illustrates by including a quote from Boyne's website, is that "'a fable' is a piece of fiction that contains a moral." The Point writer of the opposing essay had previously argued that by labeling *The Boy in the Striped Pajamas* a fable, Boyne acknowledged that it was not intended to be a realistic historical account but rather a piece of fiction with a valuable moral lesson. As we will see, however, the Counterpoint writer uses the same information presented by the Point writer to refute the validity of both Boyne's and the Point writer's reasoning and to support his own claim:

> Personally, I don't like fables. But that aside, **the problem with Boyne's premise is that writing a fable does not release him from an author's obligation not to distort history. This is particularly true when dealing with an event as serious as the Holocaust.** The danger of "serving the story" over serving the facts is that young readers will not know enough Holocaust history to understand what has been changed. As critic David

Cesarani notes, "Except for a few peculiar cases there were no Jewish children in the extermination camps: they were gassed on arrival" (Cesarani). Thus the very premise of the story is, in Cesarani's words, "utterly implausible." **In his scathing review of the book, Cesarani explains why the implausibility matters:** "Should this matter if the book is a 'fable' which is presumably intended by its author to warn against the evils of prejudice? Yes. Because there are people at large who contest whether the systematic mass murder of the Jews occurred" (Cesarani). **This is a serious charge, especially given that, according to Boyne's website, the book has sold more than 6 million copies worldwide and has been made into a movie (Boyne).**

Although the paragraph begins with a personal opinion that is not relevant to the argument and should not be included ("Personally, I don't like fables"), it presents strong reasoning and evidence for the writer's claim and effectively distinguishes the writer's claim from the opposition. The evidence comes mainly from quotations from respected critic David Cesarani, who argues that the premise of the *The Boy in the Striped Pajamas* is "utterly implausible" and that this implausibility matters because there are still people who deny the reality of the Holocaust. The Counterpoint writer then cites statistical evidence also cited by the Point writer to show why it supports his claim more than hers: the fact that the book has sold over six million copies and been made into a movie is less evidence of its merit than proof of its threat.

Then, to counter the Point writer's evidence about critical praise for the book, the Counterpoint writer provides evidence of critical condemnation:

> **The critics of the book and the 2008 movie are many. One of their complaints is Boyne's use of clever word devices to avoid addressing the real facts of the Holocaust.** Young Bruno mishears "Auschwitz" as "Out-With" and "the Führer" as "the Fury." **As Cesarani points out, "Any normal German nine-year-old would have been able to pronounce Führer and Auschwitz correctly."** While not anachronistic in the sense of being from the wrong time, Bruno's word choices are culturally misplaced. **As reviewer A. O. Scott notes, "There is something illogical about them, since Bruno's native language is presumably German, in which the portentous puns would make no sense, not English, in which they do" (Scott).**

The writer supports the main idea or reason in this paragraph—that Boyne's word devices enable him to avoid addressing real facts about the Holocaust—with evidence in the form of direct quotations from two critics that point out an inherent lack of logic in Boyne's method.

PRACTICE

In the last lesson, you created a chart to help you organize your writing. Use that information for this exercise. You will also need highlighting markers in three different colors. Follow these steps:

- On your chart, categorize the details according to their type (facts, examples, research, quotations, conclusions, definitions). You can mark these in different ways if you have fewer than three colors for highlighting. For example, you could highlight the quotations in yellow and underline the definitions in yellow. Categorize each piece of information.

- Look at your highlights. How colorful is your organizer? Ideally, the colors should be somewhat balanced, with no one color dominating the paper. This means that you have a variety of supporting details that will grab your readers' attention and hold their interest.

- Next, evaluate your details for relevance and value. Rate each one on a scale of 1 to 3. Details with a rating of 1 should be the most relevant and the most valuable. Those with a rating of 2 should be somewhat relevant and somewhat valuable. Put a rating of 3 on any details that no longer seem relevant or valuable. Hopefully, you were able to rate most of your details at level 1. A few level 2 details can be used in your paper if you need to, but all of the level 3 details should be excluded. You may find that you need to return to the research step to find more information if you had a number of details that had a rating of 2 or 3.

- When you feel that most of your details are rated 1 and that you have a wide variety of information as reflected by the highlighting, exchange your work with a peer and give each other some feedback. Check your peer's work for a balance of supporting details. Make sure most of the details are rated a 1, meaning they are relevant and valuable. Be sure to keep your feedback constructive, positive, and polite.

NOTES

PLAN

CA-CCSS: CA.W.8.1a, CA.W.8.1b, CA.W.8.5, CA.W.8.6, CA.W.8.9b, CA.SL.8.1a, CA.SL.8.1c, CA.SL.8.1d

WRITING PROMPT

Carefully consider the selections you have read in this unit, including their themes and the ideas they offer about war and conflict. Pick two of the selections from the unit and write an argumentative essay that presents a claim in answer to the following question: how can people best respond to conflict? Along with information from the selections, include research from at least three other credible print and digital sources to support your claim and develop your argument.

Your argumentative essay should include:

- An introduction with a clear thesis statement that presents your claim
- Organized body paragraphs with relevant evidence and support for your claim as well as clear transitions to show the connections among ideas
- A concluding paragraph that effectively wraps up your essay
- A Works Cited page that, in addition to the two unit texts, lists at least three other reliable sources used in your essay

You have already created an *Organize Argumentative Writing Three-Column Chart* graphic organizer. You will use the information you recorded there to plan your argumentative essay. This three-column chart contains your claim, reasons that reinforce your claim or types of support you plan to use to reinforce your claim, and examples of evidence from each source that will convince the reader to adopt your point of view on the issue. This chart, along with your thesis statement, will help you create a "road map" that will, in turn, help you write your essay.

Please note that excerpts and passages in the StudySync® library and this workbook are intended as touchstones to generate interest in an author's work. The excerpts and passages do not substitute for the reading of entire texts, and StudySync® strongly recommends that students seek out and purchase the whole literary or informational work in order to experience it as the author intended. Links to online resellers are available in our digital library. In addition, complete works may be ordered through an authorized reseller by filling out and returning to StudySync® the order form enclosed in this workbook.

Reading & Writing Companion 109

Think about the following questions as you develop reasons and organize evidence to support your thesis statement in your road map. The answers to the questions will help you to plan the content for each body paragraph of your argumentative essay:

- In what order should you present your claims and supporting details? How do they naturally build on one another?
- What reason forms the next step in your argument?
- What pieces of evidence drawn from research will convince your reader to agree to your claim?
- How can you organize the evidence so that each piece forms a foundation for the next?
- What will make your argument more convincing?
- How can you acknowledge alternate or opposing claims and distinguish your own position from these?
- Through what logical steps can you guide the reader to agree that your main thesis and supporting claims are correct?

The author of the Student Model, "Attitude: One Secret to Survival," created this road map before she wrote her essay. Use this model as an example to get started with your own road map:

Argumentative Essay Road Map

Introductory paragraph: Present the topic with the hook of the history of cruelty between humans. Provide examples of the Nazi concentration camps and Japanese internment camps. Thesis statement (claim): Positive thinking is one of the best ways to respond to conflict, as well as an effective path to healing for those who survive physical abuse or hardship at the hands of others.

> Body Paragraph 1 Topic: Examples from primary sources, including diaries and letters, of the impact of a positive attitude on survival in harsh circumstances
>
> > Supporting Detail #1: Anne Frank, quote about decorating walls, detail about chiming clock, shows engagement and positive attitude
> > Supporting Detail #2: Louise Ogawa, beauty of river, novelty of eating weenies with knife, shows engagement and positive attitude
> > Supporting Details #3 and #4: To address an alternate or opposing claim about the ultimate significance of Anne Frank's positive attitude: Statistics about the number of languages into which her

Copyright © BookheadEd Learning, LLC

diary has been translated and the number of people who have visited her home since it opened as a museum in Amsterdam in 1960

Body Paragraph 2 Topic: Scholars' analysis of the relationship between attitude and survival

Supporting Detail #1: FCIT: music and Holocaust, too many lyrics for existing tunes, "so hungry I can't sing . . . that's why you must" quotation
Supporting Detail #2: Schaumann quote about the connection between attitude and survival
Body Paragraph 3 Topic: Experts' opinions about the relationship between attitude and survival
Supporting Detail #1: Lawson quotes: positive emotions reverse negative effects and gratitude improves physical well-being
Supporting Detail #2: Lawson conclusion: focus on positive leads to resilience

Concluding paragraph: Summarize—attitude is necessary to healthy living and survival, and it creates resilience. Anne Frank and Louise Ogawa are examples that inspire. Positive attitudes contribute to the emotional resilience necessary for survival in harsh conditions.

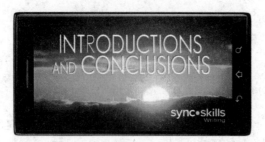

SKILL:
INTRODUCTIONS
AND
CONCLUSIONS

 DEFINE

The **introduction** is the opening paragraph or section of a nonfiction text. In an argumentative text, the introduction sets the stage for reading by **introducing the topic** or issue, **introducing the main sources** of information, and stating the **thesis or claim** in which the author takes a clear position on an issue. A strong introduction grabs the reader's attention with a **hook.** This can be a question, a startling fact or statistic, an engaging example, or a controversial statement.

The **conclusion** is the ending paragraph or section of an essay. In an argumentative text, the conclusion reviews the thesis or claim and **the most important evidence** that the writer has presented to support the claim. A good conclusion wraps up the case for the claim, showing why the reader should agree with the writer. The author restates the thesis in the conclusion and ends with a strong **call to action** or other statement that will leave a **lasting impression** on the reader.

 IDENTIFICATION AND APPLICATION

- The introduction of an argumentative paper begins with a **hook** that will immediately grab the reader's attention. There are a number of strategies for doing this, including:
  › Asking a question
  › Presenting a startling fact or statistic
  › Making a controversial statement
  › Relating an anecdote or example

- The introduction clearly tells the reader what the **topic** of the essay will be.

NOTES

- The introduction can sometimes be used to introduce the main **sources** of information that the writer will use later for **supporting evidence.**
  - › The title and author should be included in the **reference.** Sources can also be people or examples the author plans to discuss.

- The introduction includes the author's **claim** or **thesis** near the end. This is the main idea of the essay, which the author plans to **prove** to be true. The claim statement should express a clear **point of view** on the issue discussed in the essay. This statement is very important because it controls the direction of the entire essay.
- Every argumentative essay ends with a **conclusion** that summarizes the evidence the author has offered to support the claim.
- The conclusion effectively brings the argument to a close and leaves no room for doubt that the author has proved the point in the claim. It should restate the thesis and review the strongest evidence that supports the main idea.

 MODEL

Look at the introduction from the Point essay "The Value of Teaching History Through Fiction" in *Teaching History Through Fiction.*

> **Every history teacher knows that making students believe that history is relevant to their lives is Challenge Number 1. The question is, how can this difficult feat be accomplished?** One answer lies in a source we might least expect: fiction. As Valerie Tripp points out in her blog entry on the teachinghistory.org website, "Fiction can make history matter—make it irresistible—to young readers" (Tripp). This effect is achieved by John Boyne's *The Boy in the Striped Pajamas.* By approaching the Holocaust through the eyes of two nine-year-old boys, the book provides a unique perspective on this dark and horrible chapter in history. **Fiction, including stories, novels, and films, is a great way to teach people about history, and John Boyne's *The Boy in the Striped Pajamas* is an excellent example.**

The first two sentences of the Point essay provide a hook for readers. The first sentence identifies the main problem every history teacher faces: making history relevant for students. This is a relevant concern for her academic audience. The second sentence asks how this problem can be solved, which provokes curiosity and leads both teachers and students to read on to find the answer.

In the next sentence, the Point writer gives the answer: fiction. She provides support for this perhaps surprising idea in the form of a quote. To illustrate the point made in the quote, she then provides a specific example—namely, that John Boyne's *The Boy in the Striped Pajamas* offers a unique perspective on the Holocaust.

The final sentence is the Point writer's thesis statement. She clearly states her position on the controversial issue of whether fiction is an effective vehicle for teaching history and identifies the text she will analyze to demonstrate the validity of her claim: that fiction is a great way to teach people about history, and that *The Boy in the Striped Pajamas* is an excellent example.

Now read the conclusion from the same essay:

> *The goal of good fiction should be to move people. It should move them to laugh, to cry, to care, to think—or else why should they bother reading it? History too should move people—or else how will they learn from it? By exploring the moral issues of the Holocaust through the eyes of two innocent young boys,* The Boy in the Striped Pajamas *accomplishes what should be important aims of both fiction and history: it moves people to care and to think. Thus, the story is an excellent example of how to teach history through fiction.*

The first four sentences of the conclusion offer readers additional insight in the form of interesting though certainly debatable points: that both fiction and history should move people to care and to think, and that *The Boy in the Striped Pajamas* thus accomplishes what should be important aims of both fiction and history. The third sentence summarizes the author's main point about the book: that it explores moral issues related to the Holocaust. The last sentence then restates the author's thesis. In a brief space, therefore, the author summarizes her main reason, restates her central claim, and leaves readers with a lasting impression.

 ## PRACTICE

Write an introduction for your argumentative essay that begins with a hook. Then introduce the issue, your main sources, and end with a clear thesis statement. When you have finished, write a conclusion for your essay. Summarize the strongest evidence supporting your claim. Restate the thesis statement, and leave the reader with a convincing argument to share your opinion on the issue. When you are finished, trade with a partner and offer each other feedback. Does the hook capture the reader's attention effectively? Are the topic and main sources clearly introduced? Does the thesis statement make a clear claim about the issue? Does the concluding paragraph follow from and support the claim introduced in the introduction? Offer constructive suggestions to your partner and remember to phrase everything in kind and helpful ways.

NOTES

DRAFT

CA-CCSS: CA.W.8.1a, CA.W.8.1b, CA.W.8.1c, CA.W.8.1d, CA.W.8.1e, CA.W.8.4, CA.W.8.5, CA.W.8.6, CA.W.8.7, CA.W.8.8, CA.W.8.9b, CA.W.8.10, CA.L.8.2a

WRITING PROMPT

Carefully consider the selections you have read in this unit, including their themes and the ideas they offer about war and conflict. Pick two of the selections from the unit and write an argumentative essay that presents a claim in answer to the following question: how can people best respond to conflict? Along with information from the selections, include research from at least three other credible print and digital sources to support your claim and develop your argument.

Your argumentative essay should include:

- An introduction with a clear thesis statement that presents your claim
- Organized body paragraphs with relevant evidence and support for your claim as well as clear transitions to show the connections among ideas
- A concluding paragraph that effectively wraps up your essay
- A Works Cited page that, in addition to the two unit texts, lists at least three other reliable sources used in your essay

You have already started writing your own argumentative essay. You have considered your purpose, your audience, and your topic. You have examined the texts featured in the unit and developed your claim. You have also located at least three outside reliable sources and have taken notes about the ideas they contain that support your claim. You know what you want to say about this topic and the stand you are prepared to take. You have already developed a plan for organization and gathered supporting details. You've drafted several paragraphs, including the introduction and conclusion. You have considered how to achieve a formal style and to use transitions appropriately. Now it is time to write a complete draft of your essay.

Use your outline, your notes, graphic organizers, and any other pre-writing materials that you have developed to help you write this draft. Remember that argumentative writing begins with an introduction that presents a claim about the topic in a sound thesis statement. Body paragraphs add substance to the claim by adding information drawn from research, including expert opinions, examples, details, and quotations. In your essay, these paragraphs will also contain information from the selections in the unit that will help support your claim. Include carefully chosen transitions to help build your case and convince the reader that your position is the correct one. Transitions will help clarify the relationship between your ideas and the evidence you've chosen to support them. Finally, a concluding paragraph should restate or reinforce your thesis statement or claim. Your reader should be left with a clear understanding of your position and how strongly it is supported. An effective conclusion will complete the job of convincing your reader that your claim is valid.

When drafting, ask yourself these questions:

- How can I make my hook in the introduction exciting or interesting in order to capture the reader's attention?
- What can I do to explain and clarify my thesis statement or claim?
- What textual evidence—including relevant facts, strong details, and interesting quotations in each body paragraph—supports my thesis statement or claim and thus helps achieve my purpose? Be sure to include information drawn from at least three reliable sources obtained during research, clearly and accurately citing the ideas from those authors in order to avoid plagiarism.
- How logical and effective is my organizational structure?
- Have I used transitions to connect the ideas and information in my essay?
- In what ways do I distinguish my claim from alternate or opposing claims?
- Can I make the text more interesting, exciting, or vivid by using more specific language or different details?
- In what ways can I improve my style to make it more formal and appropriate for an argumentative essay?
- Have I used dashes appropriately?
- How well did I relate the stories I have chosen for this essay? Did I explain how people responded to conflict or survived their situations?
- What final thought do I want to leave with my readers?

Before you submit your draft, read it over carefully. Be sure you have responded to all parts of the prompt.

SKILL:
SOURCES AND
CITATIONS

 DEFINE

Sources are the documents and information that an author locates through research. They add authority and support to argumentative writing. They also provide the proof that an author's claim is correct. A **primary source** is an actual record of something that has survived from the past, such as a document or objects such as photographs or clothing. **Secondary sources** are accounts of the past created by people writing about events sometime after they took place.

Whether they use primary or secondary sources, authors must clearly identify where their information comes from. They do this by providing **citations,** or notes about the author or speaker and the publication or place where the information originated. Citations give credit for quotations or any ideas that did not come from the essay writer. In the body of the paper, the author often uses **in-line citations.** These give the name of the source and, if possible, the page number where the information can be found. In-line citations are placed in parentheses at the end of a sentence containing a quotation or an idea from another person. At the end of the paper, the **Works Cited** section forms a bibliography that gives complete information about each source. It allows readers to locate the source for further review.

 IDENTIFICATION AND APPLICATION

- Primary sources are the most convincing and respected sources in an argument. Primary sources are actual records of something that have survived from the past. They can include:
  › Letters
  › Diaries or journals
  › Photographs
  › Official documents
  › Artifacts
  › Memoirs

Copyright © BookheadEd Learning, LLC

NOTES

> Autobiographies
> Firsthand accounts and interviews
> Audio recordings, video recordings, or media broadcasts
> Works of art

- Secondary sources, interpretation and analysis of primary sources, are usually text. They provide expert opinions about the ideas, events, or accounts in primary sources. Some examples of secondary sources include:

  > Encyclopedia articles
  > Textbooks
  > Commentary or criticisms
  > Histories
  > Documentary films
  > News analyses

- All sources must be credible, or trustworthy, and accurate. Writers of argumentative text use primary source information whenever possible, as well as discussion and analysis from experts. Return to the Skills lesson on Research and Note-Taking to review guidelines for credible sources.

- Direct quotations from other people always need to be cited. The words must appear within quotation marks to show that the phrase, sentence, or selection came from another person. The words should be reproduced exactly as the source stated them, and the author should include an in-line citation to show the source of the text.

- Argumentative essay writers must also give credit for ideas that come from other sources, even if they are not quoted exactly. The essay author must cite paraphrased ideas.

 MODEL

The writer of the Student Model has used quotations in this excerpt. She has also paraphrased some information, and placed citations in parentheses to show where the information came from.

The impact of a positive attitude is shown in the thoughts and words of real people depicted in literature. In Anne Frank: The Diary of a Young Girl, *Anne's accounts reveal a positive attitude that later served as inspiration for millions of people.* **For example, in her diary entry dated Saturday, July 11, 1942, even while living in crowded, difficult conditions while hiding from the Nazis—worried that the entire family might be discovered at any time— Anne notes that "Thanks to Father – who brought my entire postcard and** movie-star collection here beforehand — and to a brush and a pot of glue, I was able to plaster the wall with pictures. It looks much more cheerful" (Frank 20). She also writes of the everyday details of her life, such as the chiming of the clock near their hidden location. **A similar example from a different situation comes from a Japanese internment camp in the United States from the same period. In** *Dear Miss Breed: True Stories of the Japanese American Incarceration During World War II and a Librarian Who Made a Difference,* **Louise Ogawa writes to Miss Breed about the beauty of the Colorado River they had crossed on their way to the incarceration camp. Louise showed that she was trying to find positive things to think about when she wrote, "Yesterday, I ate rice, weenies, and cabbage with a knife. That was a new experience for me!" (Oppenheim 114).** These two individuals show that they were trying to keep a positive attitude in extremely difficult circumstances. Although some may argue that a positive attitude didn't really help Anne Frank, who ended up dying in the Bergen-Belsen concentration camp, her strength and spirit while enduring tremendously difficult circumstances have inspired countless individuals across the decades. **The diary has been translated into 70 languages, and over 28 million people have visited her home since it opened as a museum in 1960 (The Anne Frank House).** Her positive attitude therefore has had a profound impact beyond her own life and cannot be discounted.

Before each sentence that includes a quotation, the student writer's own words introduce the source. The text appearing in quotation marks is exactly the same as the text of the source from which it was taken. The student writer did not change any words or punctuation. The student author also cited the source author's name and a page number in parentheses after each quote. In addition, the student writer gave credit to statistical information she paraphrased from a credible website through another parenthetical citation.

In the "Works Cited" list at the end of the essay, the writer has provided all the essential information about works she used in the research and preparation of her essay.

Works Cited

Frank, Anne. Anne Frank: The Diary of a Young Girl. New York: Doubleday, 1952.

Copyright © BookheadEd Learning, LLC

NOTES

Lawson, Karen, M.D. "How Do Thoughts & Emotions Impact Health?" *Taking Charge of Your Health and Well-Being.* University of Minnesota. Web. 12 Dec. 2014. http://www.takingcharge.csh.umn.edu/enhance-your-wellbeing/health/thoughts-emotions/how-do-thoughts-emotions-impact-health

"Music of the Ghettos and Camps." *A Teacher's Guide to the Holocaust.* The Florida Center for Instructional Technology, College of Education, University of South Florida. C. 1997–2013. Web. 12 Dec. 2014.   http://fcit.coedu.usf.edu/holocaust/arts/musVicti.htm

Oppenheim, Joanne. *Dear Miss Breed: True Stories of the Japanese American Incarceration During World War II and a Librarian Who Made a Difference.* New York: Scholastic, Inc., 2006.

Schaumann, Caroline. "Factors Influencing Survival during the Holocaust." *History in Dispute, Vol. 11: The Holocaust, 1933–1945.* Benjamin Frankel, ed. St. James Press, 1999. Web. 12 December 2014. http://www.google.com/url?sa=t&rct=j&q=&esrc=s&source=web&cd=1&ved=0CCMQFjAA&url=http%3A%2F%2Ffacweb.northseattle.edu%2Fcadler%2FGlobal_Dialogues%2FReadings%2FMaus_Readings%2FFactors%2520Influencing%2520Survival%2520during%2520the%2520Holocaust.doc&ei=YT-LVKuOKYqOyQSCpoCoDQ&usg=AFQjCNEoEdrB6D18vVuQyPy96REwrVu1mQ&sig2=Ui_cnN68CkQxmdGvtLNPWA&bvm=bv.81828268,d.aWw&cad=rja

Virtual Museum of The Anne Frank House. Anne Frank Stichting. 28 April 2010. Web. 27 March 2015. http://www.annefrank.org/en/subsites/timeline/postwar-period-1945—present-day/the-diary-is-published/1950/the-diary-of-anne-frank-is-published-in-germany-in-an-edition-of-4500-copies-a-very-successful-paperback-edition-follows-in-1955/#!/en/subsites/timeline/postwar-period-1945--present-day/the-diary-is-published/1950/the-diary-of-anne-frank-is-published-in-germany-in-an-edition-of-4500-copies-a-very-successful-paperback-edition-follows-in-1955/

http://www.annefrank.org/en/News/Press/Visitor-numbers/

Notice that all the works referenced in the essay are listed here. For each work cited, complete bibliographic information is presented including the author's name, the title of the work, the place of publication, the publisher, and the date of publication.

It is common practice to present the titles of full-length works such as books, plays, and movies in italics. Shorter works, such as titles of articles, chapters, short stories, poems, and songs are presented within quotation marks.

If you scan the items in the Works Cited list, you will see that most types of sources follow the same general sequence: author, title of the work, publication information. Commas are used to set off elements within each of these general groupings, but each grouping ends with a period. Notice how, when a source is electronic, an element of the citation indicates that the item is from the "Web." In the event that a source has no named author, the citation begins with the title of the work or the website from which information was obtained.

The style for the material presented in this Works Cited list is based on standards established by the Modern Language Association (MLA). However, there are many other acceptable forms of citation. When completing academic writing, it is important to determine if any other particular style of citation is required by your teacher.

 ## PRACTICE

Check over the draft copy of your argumentative essay that you created in the previous lesson. Look for proper citations of all quotations, ideas, and information that came from other sources. Then make sure your Works Cited page contains correct and complete bibliographical information matching all of the sources you used in your paper. When you feel your citations are complete and correct, exchange your draft with a partner to give and receive feedback.

Review one draft from a peer. Check your peer's work to see if all ideas, quotations, and other information that came from outside sources is cited correctly. Check the Works Cited page to make sure each source is listed and that each listing contains correct and complete information so that a reader could locate the source or understand where the information came from. Remember to keep your comments kind, helpful, and constructive.

REVISE

CA-CCSS: CA.W.8.1a, CA.W.8.1b, CA.W.8.1c, CA.W.8.1d, CA.W.8.1e, CA.W.8.4, CA.W.8.5, CA.W.8.6, CA.W.8.7, CA.W.8.8, CA.W.8.9b, CA.W.8.10, CA.SL.8.1a, CA.L.8.1b, CA.L.8.1d, CA.L.8.3a

WRITING PROMPT

Carefully consider the selections you have read in this unit, including their themes and the ideas they offer about war and conflict. Pick two of the selections from the unit and write an argumentative essay that presents a claim in answer to the following question: how can people best respond to conflict? Along with information from the selections, include research from at least three other credible print and digital sources to support your claim and develop your argument.

Your argumentative essay should include:

- An introduction with a clear thesis statement that presents your claim
- Organized body paragraphs with relevant evidence and support for your claim as well as clear transitions to show the connections among ideas
- A concluding paragraph that effectively wraps up your essay
- A Works Cited page that, in addition to the two unit texts, lists at least three other reliable sources used in your essay

You have written a draft of your argumentative text. You have also received input from your peers about how to improve it and learned more information about how to properly cite your sources. Now you are going to revise your draft.

Here are some recommendations to help you revise.

- Think about the suggestions you received from the peer reviews. Which ones would you like to include as you revise?
- Consider what other changes you could make to improve your essay's evidence, analysis, or organization.

NOTES

> Reread your introduction and your conclusion. Is your claim clear in both of these paragraphs? How can you improve these paragraphs?

> Reread the body paragraphs. Is your claim supported by evidence drawn from the unit texts and credible sources obtained from research? What new or additional textual evidence could you add to strengthen support for your claim? What details could you add to capture the readers' interest? For example, did you supply personal stories to serve as examples of how people cope with abusive situations in a positive manner? Could you relate an anecdote about a positive attitude in a time of war with students' lives today?

> Have you acknowledged an alternate or opposing claim and distinguished it from your own? How so?

> How effective is your organizational structure? Are ideas presented logically? Do transition words and phrases connect your paragraphs? Do the transitions that you have chosen clearly show the relationships among claims, counterclaims, reasons, and evidence? How could you strengthen your essay's flow by improving your use of transitions?

> Check for plagiarism. Did you use paraphrase and use direct quotations from your sources and give them credit in the proper format? Quotations will enliven your essay and make it more interesting for readers. Be sure to cite your sources when you use quotations.

> Is your Works Cited page correct, complete, and accurate?

> Examine your word choice and vocabulary. Can you improve your essay by choosing a more precise or vivid word instead of a less precise one?

> Have you formed and used verbs in the active and passive voice correctly to achieve particular effects?

• When you feel that your argumentative essay is complete in terms of content, examine your draft to make sure you have maintained a formal style. A formal style shows your audience the seriousness of your ideas.

> As you revise, remove any slang terms, contractions, or other informal language.

> Do not use any first-person pronouns such as *I, me,* or *my.* Do not address your readers as *you.* These terms are more suitable for informal writing, such as for letters to friends, informal descriptions, and so forth. Make sure that you have used all of the pronouns in your essay correctly.

> Look for personal opinions that do not have supporting evidence. These do not belong in formal writing based on research. Make sure your essay is clear and direct, and that all of your points are supported by facts and logical reasoning.

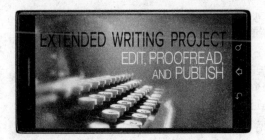

EDIT, PROOFREAD, AND PUBLISH

CA-CCSS: CA.W.8.1a, CA.W.8.1b, CA.W.8.1c, CA.W.8.1d, CA.W.8.1e, CA.W.8.4, CA.W.8.5, CA.W.8.6, CA.W.8.7, CA.W.8.8, CA.W.8.9b, CA.W.8.10, CA.SL.8.1a, CA.SL.8.3, CA.SL.8.4, CA.SL.8.4a, CA.L.8.1b, CA.L.8.1c, CA.L.8.1d, CA.L.8.2a, CA.L.8.3a

WRITING PROMPT

Carefully consider the selections you have read in this unit, including their themes and the ideas they offer about war and conflict. Pick two of the selections from the unit and write an argumentative essay that presents a claim in answer to the following question: how can people best respond to conflict? Along with information from the selections, include research from at least three other credible print and digital sources to support your claim and develop your argument.

Your argumentative essay should include:

- An introduction with a clear thesis statement that presents your claim
- Organized body paragraphs with relevant evidence and support for your claim as well as clear transitions to show the connections among ideas
- A concluding paragraph that effectively wraps up your essay
- A Works Cited page that, in addition to the two unit texts, lists at least three other reliable sources used in your essay

You have revised your argumentative essay and submitted it to your peers for review. They gave you suggestions and feedback, so you are ready to edit your essay and proofread it so it is ready to be published. Read through your essay one more time and make sure you have considered and incorporated the valuable input from the peer reviews. Reread your claim, presented in the introduction, supported in the body paragraphs, and restated in the conclusion. Did you fully develop your claim and use strong evidence drawn from sources to support your stance? Did you adequately distinguish your claim from alternate or opposing ones? Did you cite your sources accurately? Is there any way to improve the organization or transitions? Have you

Please note that excerpts and passages in the StudySync® library and this workbook are intended as touchstones to generate interest in an author's work. The excerpts and passages do not substitute for the reading of entire texts, and StudySync® strongly recommends that students seek out and purchase the whole literary or informational work in order to experience it as the author intended. Links to online resellers are available in our digital library. In addition, complete works may be ordered through an authorized reseller by filling out and returning to StudySync® the order form enclosed in this workbook.

Reading & Writing Companion **125**

maintained a consistently formal style throughout the essay? What other aspects of this essay can still be improved?

After you have thoughtfully reviewed your essay and made adjustments to strengthen it, it is time to proofread for errors. As you proofread, think about your punctuation (especially punctuation of quotations and citations and to set off nonrestrictive or parenthetical elements). Have you used dashes correctly? Did you correctly form and use verbs in the active and passive voice, and in the indicative, imperative, interrogative, conditional, and subjunctive mood to achieve particular effects, avoiding inappropriate shifts in voice or mood? Look for misspelled words, as well.

Once you have made all necessary corrections, it is time to submit and publish your work. Who might be interested in reading this piece? You may distribute your finished essay to family and friends, post it on a bulletin board, or publish it on your blog. If you do publish online, remember to create links to your online sources and citations. This will help your readers have easy access to more information about the topic.

Powered by BookheadEd Learning, LLC

Text Fulfillment Through StudySync

If you are interested in specific titles, please fill out the form below and we will check availability through our partners.

ORDER DETAILS

Date:

TITLE	AUTHOR	Paperback/ Hardcover	Specific Edition *If Applicable*	Quantity

SHIPPING INFORMATION

Contact:

Title:

School/District:

Address Line 1:

Address Line 2:

Zip or Postal Code:

Phone:

Mobile:

Email:

BILLING INFORMATION   ☐ *SAME AS SHIPPING*

Contact:

Title:

School/District:

Address Line 1:

Address Line 2:

Zip or Postal Code:

Phone:

Mobile:

Email:

PAYMENT INFORMATION

☐ CREDIT CARD

Name on Card:

Card Number: Expiration Date: Security Code:

☐ PO

Purchase Order Number:

StudySync Text Fulfillment, BookheadEd Learning, LLC
610 Daniel Young Drive | Sonoma, CA 95476